Jam Making Month-by-Month

The Jammy Bodger's Guide to Making Jam

By Mel Sellings

Jam Making Month-By-Month
The Jammy Bodger's Guide to Making Jam

Published by The Good Life Press Ltd. 2011
Copyright © Mel Sellings
Cover design by Fat Giraffe www.fatgiraphics.com
Printed by Cambrian Printers, Wales,UK

ISBN 978 1 90487 1958

A catalogue record for this book is available from the British Library.

Published by
The Good Life Press Ltd.
PO Box 536
Preston
Lancashire
PR2 9ZY
www.goodlifepress.co.uk
www.homefarmer.co.uk

THANK YOU TO

Steve, an unbeatable fruit picker with the patience of a hippo who helped me win the race, or at least made sure a flagging horse made it past the finishing post/line, or whatever the analogy is. I couldn't have done it (written the book) without you or Regula, whose fabulous fruit and vegetables got all this started, and whose endless patient help and advice led to the name Regula Guru, although she prefers just Regula... Jen for her enthusiasm, being a recipe tester, and who managed to read the whole book without mentioning all the typos and boring bits, and gave very helpful feedback. Diana at Deli for help and guidance; Colin for his photography, apples and support; Delphine, Jo, Dawn and my mum for listening; everyone featuring in the Recipe Pages, or generally in the book, Liz and Wenda for labels and chat; Dawn and Robin Beuschert for their apples; Ann and Ian Wainwright for their apples; Karen and Mrs S Wright for their plums, damsons and apples; Ben and Catherine Bowerman; Kathy and Philip at Church Knowle as I don't want to cut off my fruit supplies; Paul at Tai Chi and his mother-in-law and Sean at his work; Julia at the Fish Shop for taste testing; everyone for donating jars, recipe ideas and putting up with jam chat; everyone else for letting me mention them; Erini Constantinou for coming up with the book name; Roger for letting me type at work and Monika for her recipe page and The Good Life Press for letting me miss every deadline and not even getting narky.

Thanks to Marguerite Patten and Mrs Beeton; the old guidelines are still the best. I've just mixed and matched to what I've worked out as well.

CONTENTS

INTRODUCTION

Ahh, a night in front of the TV watching charming people pottering around quaintly overgrown gardens (overgrown with flowering weeds, not docks and other long rooted blighters), collecting mud-free home grown veg and snippets of herbs to make sumptuous meals in minutes. Your mouth waters and you imagine your transformed garden. But then PING your microwave meal is ready, you switch channels and the idyll is forgotten.

Well, this book is about how it works in real life; mud, messy kitchens, jam explosions and all. I'm Mel and in order to write this book I should live in a 16th century cottage with a large farmhouse kitchen(complete with aga, of course), surrounded by a walled garden containing every fruit bush known to man on which the sun always shines.

But I don't. I live in a small flat with my partner Steve with no garden,although we grow a few windswept herbs on the fire escape, and if I had an aga I wouldn't know what to do with it. The point is you don't need to be a 24/7 kitchen or gardening goddess to make your own jams and chutneys.

How do I know? Frankly because I'm not one, but last year I ended up making over 300 jars of jam.

Why? Well I'm not quite sure myself but I think it suddenly seemed silly not to use the free fruit all around me, and thanks to my local market garden I also had all sorts of fresh, spray-free veg available. So it became more a question of "Why Not?"

I admit jam making has taken over my life. Steve is practically banned from the flat in the summer – he brings in too much mud – and the chip shop sometimes has to provide dinner accompanied by the anguished cry of "Why won't it set?"

But I've learnt a lot in one intense year of 'jamming,' although I'm still no expert, and that's the point. Through trial and error (and not being too hard on yourself) you can make jam and chutney or whatever else you fancy. Being able to make pots of the good stuff from fruit and veg which might otherwise go to waste and surprising friends and family with gifts which they are genuinely (fingers crossed) pleased to get is pretty addictive. So although I may moan a lot when my jam is scummy and I'm sick of chopping veg for chutney, we're definitely living the good life… it's just a little different to how we might have imagined.

Mel Sellings, Dorset, 2011

EQUIPMENT

The Jam Pan

A stainless steel maslin or jam pan has a thick bottom and is ideal for making all types of preserves. Avoid ceramic, brass or older style aluminium pans, as the base isn't thick enough. Jam pans have sloping outsides and a large surface area, which encourages liquid to evaporate quickly and helps get a good boil going.

The standard size is 9 litres and prices range from £35 to £40. On the contintent you can buy them from the supermarket, but in the UK you will need to go to a hardware store, a hobby outlet, smallholder supply shop or specialist outlet.

Some people will be able to get the whole bodge together by begging and borrowing (one day, Regula, I WILL return your jam funnel), however, it's easier and cheaper to buy a complete jam-making starter kit which will come with jars and lids as well as pans and funnels.

Jars and Lids

Unless you've got a hidden stash of jars, hardware stores sell medium sized jars and lids or you can order in bulk online. In the longer term recycling your jars is the cheapest option. I put the word out and get given loads.

Getting labels off used jars can be tricky. Some simply fly off the second they touch soapy water, but others refuse to budge, so you can start being selective. Alternatively try soaking the jars overnight then attacking with a scratchy cloth and if that doesn't work then give up.

If your lids are in good condition – no nicks, rusty bits, sticky residue, stains or smells that won't go away – use them as they save a lot of faff with lid alternatives.

Most metal lids are fine when making jam but they are no good for chutney unless they have a plastic coating to prevent them from going rusty when in contact with the vinegar.

You can use wax discs and cellophane covers as an alternative to lids, but they are not good for chutneys (see page 39).

The Jam Funnel

An essential bit of kit with its extra large funnel to ensure all your jams go in the pot and not down the side.

Jelly Bag and Stand

Another essential bit of kit if you are planning to make jellies. You can improvise with a Heath Robinson type invention, but if you're planning to make loads of jellies it's a worthwhile investment. The jelly bags are cheap and last a good couple of years.

MAKING JAM
-THE BASICS

Jam is fruit cooked slowly until its skin is soft and its insides squidgy. As the fruit breaks down it releases a jellifying substance (pectin). The fruit is then mixed with sugar to both help it keep and make it taste good. When the fruity pulp is heated until it boils vigorously, a chemical reaction occurs between the pectin, sugar and acid from the fruit (called 'setting point'). This reaction makes the fruity pulp thick enough to spread on toast and prevents it from seeping out of a Victoria sandwich cake.

For anyone who hasn't made jam before it makes sense to start with the easiest jam, so after you've read the guidelines, have a look at the first jam recipes in June and find one you like the look of. I found blackcurrant jam and gooseberry and elderflower jam the easiest to make and possibly the most satisfying flavour-wise.

1. Preparing your Fruit

Weigh/measure the fruit according to the recipe.

Rinse the fruit in cold water in a colander, then scrub or just pull out any stalks or knobbly bits.

Shake the colander to drain the fruit, then either continue by dicing and slicing or place the fruit whole into the jam pan with the water.

2. Softening the Fruit

Simmer the fruit gently until the skins are softened, stirring occasionally.

Wash and dry the weighing bowl and weigh/measure the sugar.

Simmer the fruit gently to encourage all the pectin to leach out and the fruit to soften. Fruit skins won't soften after the sugar has been added, so make sure it's completely soft beforehand and taste a bit of fruit if you are unsure. Feel free to mash the fruity pulp a bit if you prefer your jam more pulpy without whole bits of fruit.

Softening the fruit should take anything from five minutes for strawberries (if you want them to keep their shape) to thirty minutes for thicker skinned goosies or sloes or a mix with eating apples. If the fruit absorbs all the water and still isn't soft, add a bit more. The amount of water is only a guideline as the toughness of fruit varies. It may sounds weird to call fruit tough, but think of it as relative and in comparison to other fruits rather than in comparison to say removing a strawberry jam stain from a white apron.

3. Sterilising & More Prep

Jars, lids, tongs, ladles, funnels and jugs all need to be really, really clean to stop any bacteria getting into the jam. After they have been washed, rinsed and drained they need to be sterilised. There are several different methods, but whichever method you choose, try to keep the jars warm until you are ready to pot the jam. If anything, I'm normally running a bit behind and I'm testing for set and sorting my lids out at the same time. I use the oven method for jars and then drop the lids and everything else into a water bath. Work out which of the following methods suits you best. I'd be tempted to use the dishwasher, if I had one.

Oven method (jars only) – stand the jars face up on an oven tray, making sure they don't touch each other or the sides of the tray so that the air can circulate around them.

Put the jars into a cold oven. This stops the jars cracking as they heat up gradually and then heat them at 110ºC (225ºF, Gas ¼) for 30 minutes. Turn the oven off, but leave the jars in the oven to keep warm. If making marmalade or chutney, put the jars in the oven about 30 minutes before you think it is time to pot.

Stove top method (jars only) – place the jars on a trivet or folded tea towel at the bottom of a medium sized but deep pan so that they don't touch the bottom of the pan or each other. Pour hot (not boiling) water over the jars, which can be either standing up or lying down, but do need to be totally immersed in the water. Boil the water for 10 minutes, then let it cool a little bit and use tongs to remove the jars. Drain them upside down on a cake rack and don't use them until completely dry. You can dry them in a low oven, but in that case you might as well use the oven method.

Water bath (for lids and utensils) – bring a small saucepan of water to the boil and drop the lids in, insides face up and push to the bottom with tongs. Leave them in the boiling water for 20 seconds, then remove using the sterilised tongs and place insides face down on a cake rack. Sterilise your ladle and funnel in the same way.

Dishwasher method – place the jars and lids upside down in the dishwasher, again not touching, and place on the hottest rinse cycle. Do not use detergent and leave in throughout the drying stage until completely dry. In all cases, be careful not to touch the rim of the jar and handle the jars with tongs or oven gloves.

4. Adding the Sugar

When the fruit is all squishy, add the sugar. Try to pour it into the middle of the pan and stir continuously until it has dissolved completely. Scrape the wooden spoon up the side of the jam pan to see if any crystals remain, and if they do, keep stirring. (If the fruit needs lemon juice to help it set, your recipe will say to add it now).

You can you use either preserving sugar or granulated. Preserving sugar has larger grains so dissolves faster, but I find granulated dissolves perfectly well and it's cheaper too. It should only be added when fruit skins are completely softened. Sugar also helps fruit keep its shape, which helps with soft fruit in a conserve, but is not ideal now, so soften your fruit first, and before adding the sugar reduce the heat, or if you've got electric, take the jam pan off the heat for a minute. Stir it constantly until dissolved, otherwise you will end up with sugar crystals in your jam. Stir until you can feel no scratchy grains and when you scrape the spoon up the side of the jam pan there are no grains there either.

A Note about Sugar

For jamming it's always granulated, but it varies in a conserve, and a marmalade or chutney may use a mixture. Here are just a few notes on the different types of sugar to help you find your way along the sugar aisle:

Golden granulated sugar is less refined than normal white granulated, and granulated is better than caster as it's less likely to stick to the bottom of the pan and burn. If possible, buy Fairtrade or organic, or at least a good brand like Billington's or Whitworth's which are available in all major stores. You can buy British beet sugar, but it's been heavily processed, so I give it a miss. I'm lucky and can buy mine from a cash and carry, which means I get it about 40p cheaper than a bag than in the supermarket, so order in bulk if you are able.

White granulated sugar is occasionally worth using to keep the colour of a pale jam. The only time I've used it is with herby jelly to keep the clarity, but it might also be good with rose-hip and apple jelly and green gooseberries (although they are sometimes pinky).

Preserving sugar doesn't actually contain added pectin, but it does have very large grains to help the sugar dissolve quicker, but there's not much point to this as the sugar is going to dissolve anyway, and it's more expensive.

Dark Muscovado sugar, sometimes called soft dark brown sugar, is darker, sweeter and less processed. It can be used to add a rich flavour and colour to chutneys and is sometimes added 50:50 with a white sugar to make a richer marmalade. Try to get unrefined cane sugar (it should say this clearly on the pack), as sometimes what seems to be a brown sugar is actually white processed sugar with the molasses added back in.

Light, soft brown sugar is sometimes used in chutneys because of its light molasses flavour. Annoyingly, it's only available here in 500g bags, but I do still use it as I like the added flavour and colouring.

Demerara sugar has large crystals and is crunchy and great sprinkled on top of crumbles.

Jam sugar contains added pectin to boost a low pectin jam. There are 3 other types of added pectin: liquid pectin, pectin stock and pectin sachets, but don't worry about this now, as if a recipe needs this sugar, or any other types of added pectin, it will clearly tell you.

5. Setting Point

Increase the heat to high, stop stirring and remove the spoon. The jam is setting when it is boiling all over the surface and the bubbles make a 'put, put, put' sound as they burst. It will also keep boiling when stirred. The jam is now close to 'setting point,' so remove the pan from the heat and test for set.

Jam sets at 105°C / 220°F, or slightly lower if the pectin is really high.

6. Testing for Set

Test 1 – using a wooden spoon / tablespoon, scoop up some jam out of the pan and hold it away from the rising heat. Let it cool for about 20 seconds, then turn it on its side above the jam pan. If the jam drips off like water, return the pan to the heat and continue to boil, but if it runs together and drips off in a jelli-fied lump or two it is starting to set, so move on to Test 2.

Test 2 – the saucer test. Place a tablespoon of jam on a sau-cer from the fridge, leave it for 1 minute and then draw your finger through it. If the jam wrinkles and stays separate it is set, but if not, return the pan to the heat for another couple of minutes, then test again. When you are happy with the set keep the jam pan off the heat.

7. Scum Skimming

Resist skimming the scum or foam until after the jam has reached setting point and take the wooden spoon out if scum is building up on it. Skim by stir-ring in one direction and scrap-ing the spoon over the surface and up and out of the pan. I tap the scum off on the testing saucers and then dip the spoon into a saucepan of boiling water before skimming some more. The lighter the colour of the jam, the more scum you will have to remove as it shows up in the jam, and when you are finished, stir the jam to evenly disperse the fruit. If you have large pieces of fruit in the jam, let it settle for another 10 min-utes and stir again.

Alternatives to the skimming spoon are to rub butter around the inside of the pan before starting or to add a knob of but-ter with the sugar or at setting point. Adding butter will reduce the time it keeps and is not an option for jellies as it makes them cloudy. You could also dab any bits off with kitchen roll (a bit of a faff) or use a spe-cial slotted skimming spoon, but these are rather large and clumsy.

So what is the fruity scum and what causes it? Could it be eradicated from the jam mak-er's world? Some say it's the

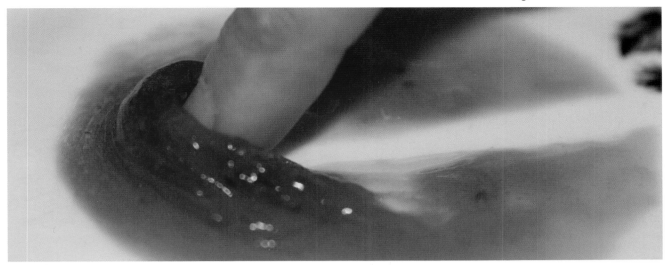

speed of cooking which causes bubbles, but I think that's more the foam. Scum seems to be more a part of the fruit structure which sets quicker when broken down. Either way, scum is here to stay, but it doesn't affect the taste of the jam, it just doesn't look good.

8. Potting the Jam

Using a funnel or a ladle, pour the jam into the jars, filling them to just below the top, officially to within 5mm (¼ inch) of the top and usually just past the shoulder of the jar. The less space there is for air, the better, although the jam will inevitably shrink back slightly as it cools down.

When all the jars are full, place the lids loosely on top, and using an oven glove, seal the lids as tightly as possible. Then place the jars on a cake rack to cool.

An alternative is to place a wax disc on top, wax side down, dampen a cellophane cover on the outside with a clean cloth, then hold it in place using a rubber band covering the mouth of the jar.

Finally, wipe the jars down, label them and store in a dark place when cold.

Prior to congratulating yourself, clean the jam pan (or if you've

had enough, just fill it with water and leave it to soak). Now congratulate yourself! Be aware too that once you've made jam a few times it gets a lot easier and you won't get into a panic worrying whether it's going to set or not... I think I'm just about getting there.

Now that you have the basics you can keep on jamming by following all the individual recipes.

MAKING CONSERVES
-THE BASICS

The star ingredient is the fruit, but now you have to care about the appearance as well as the flavour. You can't make conserves with any old fruit – only soft skinned, catwalk perfect fruit need apply. There is no chance to soften tough skins, which is a shame as you have to say good-bye to blackcurrants and gooseberries, but hello to blackberries, blueberries and cherries. Think small and perfectly formed, and if the fruit is larger like peaches or greengages they need to be clean cut and pose elegantly in the syrup.

So how Do I Make it?

Conserves seem easy to make as you do little and often over 2 or even 3 (that's you, squishy strawberries!) days. The fruit marinates in a bowl of sugar, which draws the juices out and firms the fruit. You don't want to soften the fruit, so after you've boiled it gently to dissolve the sugar you immediately bring the conserve to a steady boil, not a mad and fast boil like for jam. Pectin is often added, so there is no need to boil it for ages and risk breaking up the fruit. You must still test for set, but most conserves are a softer set, reaching approximately 104°C (219ºF), so you don't boil them forever trying to get a perfect firm set. Any alcohol or flavourings are stirred in at the end to stop them boiling off, or a larger quantity stirred in at the beginning.

There is more room for error with a conserve as you aren't looking for a rock solid set. They are all pretty easy to make and looking for an easy one to start with is less important. I made straw-

A conserve is just a posh jam, a sort of syrup with whole fruit bobbing in it, with maybe an alcoholic kick, a sprinkle of nuts, or a citrus twist to give a twizzle to your taste buds. Conserves wake up a plain cheesecake or vanilla ice cream, can be a topping for a tart, and can use up any alcohol left over from Christmas; kirsch goes with cherries, amaretto with apricots, or brandy with peaches, although absolutely nothing goes with egg-nog.

berry conserve first, which marinates for 3 days rather than 2, but is still very simple and I was really pleased with it. So choose whichever catches your eye.

Handy to Have Extras

Perhaps a large bowl to marinate the fruit in, although you could just use your jam pan for this, and something to cover it with to stop the sugary concoction attracting flying friends. The fruit is usually fine at room temperature, but if it's particularly warm you might need to pop it in the fridge. To make cherry conserve you need a cherry stoner, but the rest is standard jam making equipment.

How To Make Conserve

Day 1: Preparing the fruit

Weigh / measure the fruit, then rinse / de-stem / hull / de-stone and drain well in a colander.

Weigh / measure the sugar so that as soon as the fruit is ready you can start marinating.

Cut any larger fruit like plums or apricots in half and de-stone or halve cherries.

In a large bowl (or jam pan), layer the fruit alternately with the sugar, gently mix, cover and leave either for over 4 hours or overnight for juice extraction and fruit firming.

Day 2

Sterilise your jars and lids.

Pour the fruit and sugar into the jam pan, but be careful with the pouring as you don't want sugar stuck all over the sides of the jam pan.

Heat gently and stir until the sugar is dissolved and add any lemon juice if using.

Setting the Conserve

Heat to a steady boil until it is boiling all over the surface, just not as manic as for jam.

When it continues to boil when stirred, test for a slightly looser set than jam by the normal test 2 method, but when you drag your finger through it is ready when it wrinkles and just about stays separate. If not yet set, repeat as before.

When you are happy with the set, take the pan off the heat and stir in any alcohol or flavourings, if using them.

Skim off any scum and if it's strawberry there will be a lot.

Take your time as you really need to get it all off.

Leave the conserve to sit until it thickens slightly so that it holds the fruit in place rather than permits it to bob en masse to the surface. Stir to disperse evenly.

Potting

Pot as for jam. Store in a cool, dark cupboard, but don't forget about them: they will only keep for about 6 months.

Now you have the basics you can make conserves by following all the individual recipes.

MAKING CURDS -THE BASICS

So how Do I Make it?

Curds are quicker and easier to make than jam and there's no worrying about whether it's set or not. If you've ever melted chocolate for cooking you'll be familiar with the method for making curd, as it's made in the same way. The fruit purée or juice and zest, sugar and butter are melted in a large bowl which sits snugly on top of a saucepan of simmering water, bain marie style. The egg is added and the mixture heated until it thickens, at which point it's potted. Simples!

Home-made curds don't keep long – between one and four months depending on how much sugar you add. This doesn't matter as you only make it in small quantities. The only curd I've ever kept for 4 months was gooseberry curd which I was testing to see how long it would keep, otherwise it would have been eaten long before!

Just think of any tart fruit and you can make curd with it; blackcurrants, grapefruit, limes etc. As regards an 'easiest curd,' I would make lemon curd first. No, that's not boring, and there's a reason it's so popular. Just forget about the curd you've tasted from the shops. This is so good that certain people (who shan't remain nameless, Regula), eat it straight from the jar, whereas I take mine in a rather more dignified manner, dipped with hob-nobs.

Curd is a tart yet creamy, acidic yet buttery, fruity yet decadent treat which makes you go 'mmm!' It is wasted on toast, but comes into its own when swirled luxuriously into crème fraiche and meringue, or rippled into vanilla ice cream. OK, I've recovered from my linguistic excess now. A curd is an acidic fruit purée or juice blended with sugar for sweetness, and butter and eggs for thickness and creaminess. It just doesn't sound as good put like that!

THE JAMMY BODGER

Extras Needed

A large, heat resistant mixing bowl (curd bowl), usually glass; a medium saucepan; a sieve; a small bowl for whisking egg in; a balloon whisk (or fork); a juicer (or just sieve in the juice) and a zester (you've usually got one on a square cheese grater).

Getting Set up

Sterilise all your equipment.

CITRUS FRUIT

Weigh / measure your fruit, then rinse and give the peel a good rub and remove any knobbly or discoloured bits. If your fruit is waxed, scrub it with sugar, then rinse.

Zest the fruit straight into the curd bowl. Halve and juice your fruit, adding the juice to the curd bowl.

OTHER FRUIT (apples, gooseberries, or berries)

Weigh / measure your fruit and rinse to remove any dirt. If you've got apples, peel and chop them.

Add the fruit to a large saucepan with the water in the recipe and simmer until completely soft and mushy. Bash it with the back of the wooden spoon to help it along.

Ladle the fruity pulp into the sieve and press through with the back of a spoon into your curd bowl.

All Together Now

Bring the water beneath the curd bowl to a rapid boil with the curd bowl with the fruity stuff in sitting on top.

Weigh / measure the butter and sugar, roughly cube the butter and add it together with the sugar to the curd bowl.

Stir it, or if you've got a balloon whisk, whisk continuously until the sugar is dissolved and the butter melted.

Whisk the eggs in a small bowl, then take the curd bowl and saucepan off the heat.

Pour the eggs through the sieve into the curd bowl.

Push through the sieve with a tablespoon, then scrape the bottom to make sure you get all the egg through.

Stir or whisk the eggs into the fruity stuff, taking your time and waiting until it's all completely mixed.

Return the curd bowl and saucepan to the heat and stir or whisk occasionally over the simmering water.

When the curd begins to thicken, stir continuously.

When the curd is thick enough to coat the back of a wooden spoon (about 20 minutes after adding the egg), it is done. It will thicken slightly more when cooled.

Pot as for jam, but remember that your curd will only keep for a couple of months.

MAKING MARMALADE -THE BASICS

How Do I Make It?

There are a couple of different ways to make marmalade, but the objectives are always the same. You need soft sliced peel that flavours the water along with the juice of the fruit. You then add plenty of sugar, increase the heat and look to set. What could be difficult about that? Errr... for me a lot, but more about that later.

Marmalade has been a steep learning curve, but I have learnt a number of things. Start with a lemon marmalade and pre-soak it finely sliced, or go for the original, the marmalade which is still in a league of its own, Seville orange marmalade.

Marmalade recipes differ on how to soften the fruit and the best way to deal with the pith and pips. The two methods I've used differ on whether to slice the fruit before or after cooking. Method 1 slices the fruit first, and pre-soaking the fruit makes the difference between a chewy inedibleness and a tangy delight. Method 2 cooks the fruit whole and you just need to take your time and go slow.

Extras

A jam pan lid or silver foil; a fruit scrubbing brush or cloth and sugar; a sharp knife; a sieve, if possible nylon as it's less likely to taint the flavour; a juicer (a plastic hand one is fine) and a slotted spoon if following method 2.

You will also need a completely different mind-

Marmalade is a thick, citrusy jelly with shreds of peel, which add both flavour and texture. It can be all things to all people: tart and tangy with a bitter edge, sweet and comforting, chunky, or finely shredded and elegant. Jelly marmalades are marmalades for the faint hearted who might like the flavour but not the teeth tickling chewiness of a normal marmalade. It is an old British (I think that covers its claimed Scottish origins) favourite, and for good reason as the citrus twang lifts the heavy winter potato and parsnip palate to brighten up a dull morning.

set to making jam. Go slowly and gently; a good marmalade is like a fine wine, so I'm told, and cannot be rushed, which is probably why I wasn't very good at it as I prefer a cheap cider.

The Slice & Pre-soak Method

Day 1

Weigh, de-button and rinse the fruit, gently scrubbing away any discoloured or dirty bits. If your fruit has been waxed, scrub it with a little bit of sugar to remove the coating, and then rinse well.

Halve the fruit, squeeze the juice and sieve it into the jam pan. Measure and add the water.
Bin any pips hiding in the fruit shell using your thumb to rub them out.

Cut the halved fruit in half again, so that it's now in quarters and hold it peel side down whilst you slice horizontally close to the peel to remove the pulp. Chop up the pulp, remembering a pip check, and add it to the jam pan.

Slice the peel finely, taking your time, and add it to the jam pan.

Leave it to soak for a couple of hours or overnight if possible, covered with a lid or silver foil.

Day 2

Bring the 'peely' juice in the jam pan to the boil, then reduce the heat and simmer, covered or uncovered, depending on the recipe.

Simmer gently until the peel has softened. This takes at least a couple of hours, so again, don't rush.

Taste the peel. It's really bitter, but you are checking for texture; when it's soft enough to eat without chewing and squidges between your fingers with no resistance, it's ready.

Sterilise your jars and lids.

Adding the Sugar

When the peel is soft, weigh / measure your sugar.

Reduce the heat and stir in the sugar (and sieve in the lemon juice, if using).

Stir constantly until all the sugar has dissolved.

Setting Point

Increase the heat until it is boiling vigorously. It won't boil quite as manically as jam, but start testing for set when it is boiling fast and continuously all over the surface, and carries on boiling when stirred; you can hear the bubbles bursting with a 'put, put, put' sound, and it's getting louder; it's been boiling steadily, but is now boiling just that bit quicker, and is thickening slightly around the sides of the jam pan. The signs aren't as obvious as with jam, so test early rather than late.

As soon as you think it might be set, whip the pan off the heat and test for set. If using a sugar thermometer marmalade sets at about 105°C (220°F), or slightly lower if the fruit pectin content is really high.

Scum Skimming

There won't be loads, but it's tricky as it sticks to the peel. Do as for previous recipes, but with extra caution. You may lose a few bits of peel, but don't worry.

Leave it to Settle

Leave the marmalade to sit without stirring until it thickens slightly and there is a slight skin on the top. This should take 10-15 minutes. If it hasn't thickened after 15 minutes, test again for set, and if it's not yet ready return to the heat and

boil again. You've probably just missed set. If it has thickened, stir gently to disperse the peel evenly.

Potting is as before, as is cleaning the jam pan, whether by means of the cleaning fairy or marigolds. Label the following day when cool and store somewhere dark. Marmalade will keep for 1-2 years, depending on the amount of sugar used.

The Whole Fruit Method

This is all done in one day, so pick a day when you are pottering around the house as this is more of a little and often approach.

Weigh the fruit, then de-button and rinse and scrub gently to remove any dirt. If it's waxed, scrub gently with sugar and rinse.

Place the fruit in the jam pan with the water and bring to the boil.

Reduce the heat to a gentle simmer, covered or uncovered, for about three hours, depending on the recipe.

Turn the fruit occasionally as it bobs about on top of the water and isn't always completely submerged.

The fruit is ready when it can be pierced easily with a fork and if you lift one out and pinch it with your fingers there should be no resistance; it should almost feels as though it's empty. Remove the fruit from the water using a slotted spoon and place it on a chopping board. Pinch off a bit of the peel and taste it. It should definitely not be chewy!!

Juice and Slice

Slice the fruit in half and leave it to cool for about twenty minutes until it's easy to handle.

Gently juice the halves and place the juice and any pulp stuck around the juicer back into the jam pan. Sieve it in if your fruit has pips and check the fruit halves for hidden pips. If you find any, bin them.

Chop up any remaining fruity pulp and add it to the pan, binning any really stringy bits that might be hanging around where the top and tail were done.

Place the peel, pith side up, on a chopping board. If it still looks fat with pith, gently scrape the knife horizontally underneath the pith and put it to one side to bin later.

Finely slice the peel if you can. It's more difficult as it's damp, so small chunks are fine. Just remember it's you who will be eating them!! Add them to the jam pan.

Sterilising your jars and lids is a repeat performance and should by now be second nature.

Adding the Sugar

Heat the fruity pulp and when it is simmering gently, add the sugar and lemon juice, if using. Stir until the sugar has completely dissolved.

Setting point is a repeat performance, as is scum skimming, allowing the marmalade to settle, and potting.

Respect to the Orange

I first tried to make marmalade in the same way as jam, following all the rules, but a little slap dash, and certainly not taking enough notice of anything concerning technique. My efforts failed, and quite dismally. I just couldn't get the peel soft, and even when staring avidly into a boiling jam pan I couldn't tell if it was setting or not. It just didn't behave like jam.

So respect to the marmalade. It nearly beat me, but at the last minute I grasped that all oranges are equal, but some oranges are more equal than others: organic oranges are not easy to get hold of, but as you are using the peel it's definitely worth the effort; unwaxed are the next best as you won't have to scrub hard to remove the waxy coating, which you definitely won't want to eat, and Seville oranges have a flavour that sweet oranges can only dream of, and most are unwaxed. Mixed citrus fruit marmalades create the next best tangy alternative.

Let's Talk Peel

A lot of marmalade recipes include the faff of placing the fruity pith and pips into a muslin bag, which is added to the pan and cooked with the peely juice. It seems pretty pointless, so I stopped using it. This isn't to say I didn't have the initial problems setting marmalade, it just turned out that a little muslin bag wasn't the answer.

Setting Point

Q. When is a setting point not a setting point?

A. When making marmalade

It takes longer to set marmalade than jam, and it hovers around setting point for a while before finally giving in.

Is it setting? If you've been looking at the boiling mass for a while, and suddenly there are more bubbles and it's boiling faster and louder, and it's a little thicker around the edge, and you've probably tested it for set 2 or 3 times already, or it sounds like it's set... with marmalade you need to test early and often, so be prepared to be popping the saucers in and out of the fridge a couple of times. Setting point is easily missed and if it has passed the marmalade won't set. This sounds a tad melodramatic, but just test for set early and continue testing, making sure to take the jam pan off the heat each time.

Testing For Set

It's confession time. When I took the photos showing the marmalade saucer test for set I slightly over-set the marmalade. I didn't mean to, of course. We were just doing the saucer test photo and I left the jam pan on the heat, so the saucer test photo is absolutely fine, but the marmalade I potted was very dark and over-set. I included the photos as they show the scum on marmalade to great effect. So a missed setting point makes a marmalade darker in colour, rather thick and sticky like treacle, and which tastes like boiled sweets. All is not lost, however. Marmalade tasters are a very forgiving breed. To prevent over-setting make sure that when the dollop of marmalade is being tested for set on the saucer it just needs to wrinkle when pushed, not stay completely separate.

One final thought... it's definitely worth the effort as I feel like I've grown into an adult making marmalade, as making jam is child's play in comparison.

PS. For jelly marmalades see the questions after How to Make Jelly.

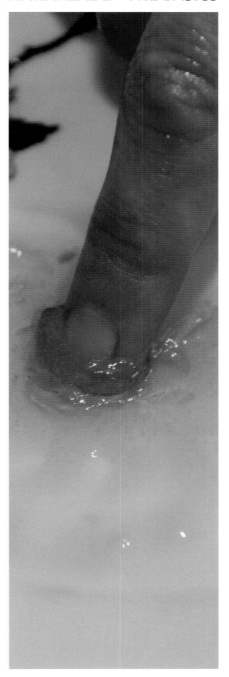

MAKING JELLY -THE BASICS

Jellies involve less initial preparation than jam. You simply chop up the fruit roughly and don't de-skin, de-stone or anything other than de-mud. The fruit is simmered slowly until it's completely pulpy and has released as much of its juice and pectin as possible. The fruity pulp is strained through a jelly bag to leave a clear juice. You then warm the juice, add the sugar and boil the jelly until it reaches setting point, testing for set as with jam. Hey presto, a seedless clear jam. Hold up a jar and watch the light shine through.

Is there an easiest first jelly? Well actually they are all about the same, but maybe start with a bramble and apple jelly in September, because jellies are usually made using a seasonal glut of fruit and there's usually a lot of both of these fruits about.

Extras

A jelly bag and stand is a must. It's simply a nylon or polyester bag hung from a stand which fits over a standard large glass bowl. They are cheap, easy to obtain and last for ages. Alternatives include using up-turned stools and old tights, but are too much faff and frankly too unpleasant to even contemplate. The legs of the jelly stand grip the bowl which catches the jelly juice as the jelly bag 'hovers' above. My large glass bowl fits great, but we have to bend the jelly stand's legs to fit a large ceramic bowl which is just a shade bigger. Wherever you buy the stand from will give you bowl size guidance, if it's anything different from the norm.

Banish any thoughts of childhood jelly. These jellies are not to be topped with custard. They are a posh jam with a beautiful silky finish that is best appreciated by adults. They can be either sweet or so tart they go great with meat, or so full bodied with an alcoholic punch which makes them an adults only treat, or so sweet that children think you are feeding them sweets, but just haven't realised.

THE JAMMY BODGER

You will also need a measuring jug, the larger the better, into which to pour the jelly juice and to measure, and a calculator, but don't panic. We aren't talking long division here, the calculator just makes it easier to work out the exact amount of sugar to add.

In addition to the usual pans and equipment you will also need some small jars and lids. You get less jars when making jelly, so switch to smaller jars and you'll find you've got more wallop for your welly.

How Much Sugar?

How much sugar you need to add is different each time you make a jelly, even if you use the same amount of fruit. Firstly, you are straining out any fruit stones, pips, skin and chewy bits, so you've always got less fruit than you started with. Secondly, how much fruity juice you get depends on how juicy or watery your fruit is this time, which is usually different to last time; your fruit may be more ripe or perhaps more stringy than juicy. You can't know how much sugar to add until after the fruit has passed through the jelly bag. The final jelly needs to be 60% sugar, so the amount of sugar needed is calculated using the formula: 450g / 2¼ cups of sugar for every 600ml / 2½ cups of juice.

Day 1: Softening your fruit

The fruit doesn't necessarily need to be peeled, or the stones or pips removed, but do rinse it well and remove any bruised or mouldy bits, then chop it up roughly.

Simmer the fruit gently as for jam. You want to slowly release as much pectin and juice as possible, but you want to go a stage further than for jam and completely pulp the fruit. You can help it along by bashing it with a wooden spoon or by using a potato masher.

Whilst the fruit is collapsing, 'scald' the jelly bag. Scalding the jelly bag simply means pouring boiling water over it and leaving it in the water to cool. When the water is cool the jelly bag is hung from the stand and the fruity pulp ladled in. 'Scalding' not only sterilises the jelly bag but makes the fruity pulp pass through it easier. I'm not exactly sure how, but take my word for it.

Now set up your jelly stand with the bag hanging from it over the bowl, somewhere it can drip through in peace without being nudged or having toast crumbs sprinkled into the juice bowl.

Filling the Jelly Bag

When the fruit is pulped, place a pan stand beside the jelly stand and place your jam pan on it.

Ladle the fruity pulp carefully into the jelly bag and if any drips straight from the ladle into the bowl you will need to pour the juice back into the jam pan and begin ladling again. (Don't worry, the jelly bag expands a lot (it looks like a swollen cow's udder). Do not give in to temptation and try to hurry the process up by pushing and prodding the bag. It will only result in a cloudy jelly!

Leave the fruity pulp to drip through the bag. This can take from a couple of hours to the whole night. I usually leave it to drip through overnight, so like a conserve it's not too much effort all at once.

Day 2

Adding the Sugar

When it has drained through, remove the jelly bag and stand from above the bowl and empty the bag into a composter, bin (or in the case of bramble and apple, keep it for making a crumble) and pour the juice into a measuring jug.

Use the ratio of 450g (1lb) of sugar for every 600ml (1 pint) of juice to work out how much sugar to add to the juice.

Making the Jelly

Pour the juice into a clean jam pan. Even if you've only got a little bit of juice, still use the jam pan as it needs room to bubble and foam.

Warm the juice gently over a low heat and when warm, pour in the sugar, stirring continuously until it has dissolved completely. If using lemon juice add it now.

Setting Point

Increase the heat to high and stop stirring. Look out for the familiar signs. Some jellies set very fast, so beware. The tests are as for earlier recipes, with the setting temperature at about 104°C (219°F), although it could be slightly lower if the pectin content is high.

Scum Skimming

With jelly you will get a LOT of scum and foam. Take care to remove as much as possible and do not rush. If you are adding herbs to the jelly, leave it to stand in the jam pan for 10 minutes after skimming before stirring in the herbs.

Potting the Jelly

Ladle or pour the jelly slowly into the jars, trying at all times to avoid any air bubbles. Otherwise the process is as earlier, and once you have wiped the jars down you can either clean the jam pan or collapse in a heap on the sofa and hope a

cup of tea materialises. You can do the labelling the day after. Well done, you've made something beautiful!

Jelly Marmalade

Jelly marmalade is like jam without the pips; it's marmalade for the faint hearted.

Peel the fruit, and if you want to add either some or all of the peel back in later, slice it finely.

Place the peel in a muslin bag tied tightly with string. The peel is bagged so it doesn't block up the jelly bag. The citrus fruit is then treated like a normal jelly with the fruit roughly chopped then simmered with the muslin bag in with it until pulpy. The bag is then removed, squeezed with tongs over the jam pan and discarded. The citrus pulp is dripped through the jelly bag and the juice is made into jelly in the normal way.

If you want you can now add some of the finely sliced peel from the muslin bag to the pan, hence the name jelly marmalade.

37

MAKING CHUTNEY - THE BASICS

So How Do I Make It?

There's a lot of prep with chopping, weighing and measuring . Pop your spices in a spice bag and let them infuse into your vinegar. The vinegar lends its sharp flavour to the fruit and veg, which is balanced when the sugar is added. And then it's the long simmer which gives all the ingredients a chance to mingle. There's no testing for set; you just boil until the chutney is thick and glossy. But don't taste your chutney now. It needs to sit somewhere cool and dark to mellow for at least a month before you can sample it.

Easiest first chutney? Probably caramelised onion marmalade in July, simply because it's based on one ingredient, so eases you gently into chutney making.

Extras

You will be able to use your stainless steel jam pan, and I strongly urge you to use a long handled wooden spoon to prevent the burning hot 'spit' reaching you.

Also, only use lids from any jar that contained something acidic in a previous life,otherwise the vinegar may corrode the inside of the lid. If in doubt you just need to separate the chutney from the lid with some greaseproof paper. Cut out a circle of greaseproof paper quite a lot bigger than your jar's rim so it sticks out from under the lid, ladle the chutney in, place the grease-

Chutney is a marriage of fruit and veg, sugar and vinegar to create a thick and chunky, sweet and savoury dollop on your plate. It makes friends with cheese and ham, and is an excellent partner to the ever elegant sausage and mash. It needs to pack a punch, not necessarily with heat but with flavour that leaves your mouth tingling, and you wondering, 'Mmm... what's in that?' So what is in it?

proof circle on top and tighten the lid.

Flavouring the Vinegar

Slice the onions and measure out the vinegar.

Prepare your spices for the spice bag. Some, like coriander seeds, cardamom pods or garlic, are best given a bash in the pestle and mortar to start releasing their flavour. Tie your spices tightly into the spice bag and if there's muslin left over, trim both it and any straggly string.

Pour half the vinegar into the jam pan and add onions, garlic, any spices which are going directly into the jam pan, and the spice bag, and simmer for 15 minutes, then take off the heat. Cover and leave to infuse whilst you prepare the rest of the fruit and veg.

Chop, chop, chop and err... slice (Actually, put the radio on!).

Prepare the rest of the fruit and veg. Peel and core apples and pears, stone any plums, peel the marrow and remove

its seeds, whilst courgettes can keep both. Try to chop everything about the same size. Prepare one veg, weigh it, note its weight, then add it to the jam pan, then start on the next ingredient. Often the weight of fruit or veg in a recipe is the weight post chopping. So chop then weigh; just check the recipe. I peel apples and leave them to soak in a bowl of water with a squirt of lemon juice to stop them going brown. I then chop them when ready, place them on the weighing scales and then into the jam pan.

Add all the fruit and veg and the rest of the vinegar and simmer until the veg is soft, for at least 1 hour, but it could take two.

Turn down the heat, add the sugar and stir until dissolved, then add the raisins or dates.

Now sterilize everything.

Turn into Chutney

Increase the heat and stir frequently, so the bottom of the jam pan doesn't burn. Continue until you can draw a wooden spoon over the surface and it leaves a trail for a couple of seconds / or you scrape the spoon along the bottom and it again leaves a clear trail / or just cook it until thick and glossy with no visible liquid, in fact nearly as thick as you would like to eat it. This will take anything from 30 minutes to 1 hour, or even longer depending on how much liquid it needs to drive off.

Potting

Remove the spice bag.

Ladle the chutney into the jars, and after filling each jar, tap it

firmly on the work surface to try to encourage the chutney to settle.

Leave a little chutney in the jam pan, then come back to the first jar and examine the jar for air bubbles. If you see any, dip the knife into the jar, pierce the air bubble and slowly withdraw the knife. This makes it sound a bit like a surgical operation. This is important as trapped air causes the chutney to dry out and enables any bacteria to thrive.

Check all your jars. You might need to top the jars up with any chutney left in the jam pan. They need to be nearly full to the top and past the shoulder, as the chutney will shrink back a little.

If using greaseproof circles, place one on the top of each jar, then twist the lids on tightly.

Label and store in a dark place for at least a month before tasting.

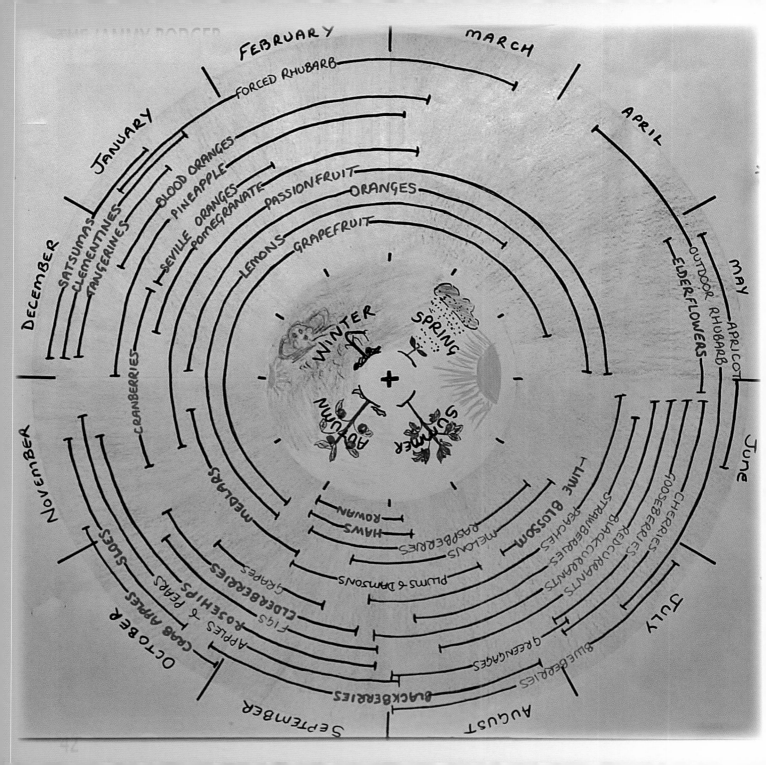

WHAT ABOUT THE FRUIT?

THE JAMMY BODGER

Fresh Is Best

I always try to find out what's in season. This isn't always easy, so there's a Seasonal Cycle on page 42 to help both you and me. It is best to use fruits which are in season, and from as close to home as possible because the fruit is:

- Fresher, so it has more flavour.

- Higher in pectin, which means it sets easier, again because the fruit is fresher.

- Cheaper as, when it's in season, there is more of it around, which keeps the cost down.

- Sprayed with less rubbish to make them keep, as they aren't travelling far, or trying to grow in unsuitable conditions.

- You get better quality as any out of season fruit will be the type of fruit which keeps longest, not which tastes best.

Where Are You, My Little Fruity?

Just look around you. There's lots of wild fruit around as well as the blackberries that everyone picks. Now don't get me wrong. I'm not being sniffy about them as they make one of my cheapest and best selling jams.

We've picked wild crab apples, elderberries, haws (I know, it sounds funny if you say it out loud), plums, rosehips, rowans and sloes. And Steve's just claimed we picked dewberries, a relative of blackberries, which look a bit like an uneven, ugly blackberry and are very squishy. All wild berries combine well with apples, which is great as apples are the fruit you are most likely to be given for free, and two free fruits make a very happy jam maker.

I'm still keeping an eye out for quinces too. Intriguingly, there's a Quince Hill 20 minutes walk away from me, but it's private. I've seen wild cherries, but they were really small and the birdies got them, and there are two overgrown and rather neglected fig trees in nearby gardens which are always very tempting.

So get to know your local area. A few places still have greengrocers, whilst others are lucky enough to have strong and thriving markets where much of the fruit and veg is sourced from local farms. Supermarkets tend to be the main source, although, surprisingly, our butchers will order fruit in for you. They were great when I was after frozen cranberries and came up trumps with Seville oranges too, so it's definitely worth asking around, even in the most surprising places.

Luckily, most of the year I get a great supply of fruit and veg from The Vege Place and a small PYO outlet, but after I've bled them dry, or the birds have, the lack of local fruit suppliers means we plan our fruit picking forays with military precision, and complete with back up plans, to a larger PYO about 10 miles away.

Pick what you Need

Do check your recipes before you go fruit picking to see how much fruit you need in kilograms. When you arrive at the PYO you can ask how much a full punnet of that fruit weighs (usually about 1kg per punnet), which gives you a rough idea of how much fruit to pick, although I always pick more than I need anyway.

You might need to be more flexible if your PYO is small. But sometimes, even with large PYOs, when you get there the strawberries might have been picked out, but the gooseberries have been neglected, or

Try to make the jam ASAP after picking the fruit, as the strawberries go squishy fast, and their pectin reduces as time passes.

they have a glut of blackcurrants so they are on a reduced offer. Pick whatever looks best fruity wise and cost wise and then find a new recipe when you get home. If anything is reduced and you can't use it now, you can always freeze it and use it later.

Supermarkets buy fruit in bulk and if it's not shifting they have to reduce it as it's got a short shelf life. Bear in mind that supermarkets often stock blander varieties of fruit chosen more for how they look and how long they keep, rather than for their flavour. But if it looks healthy and is not over-ripe, and it can make a jam you like, buy it, and buy a couple of lemons in case it's low in pectin, then go home and find an appropriate recipe.

Supermarkets can also keep you going through the winter months. If you are getting desperate for a fruity fix, check out their frozen section and have a look at April and May's recipes for some inspirational ideas.

Pick or buy your fruit when it's just ripe, or slightly under

WHAT ABOUT THE FRUIT?

ripe. Any sign of the fruit being mushy or past its prime, and it's not great for preserving; as the word suggests, you are trying to preserve the best fruit, not some knackered thing you don't even fancy eating now.

Try to pick fruit when it is dry as this helps stop mould, and try to make the preserve on the same day you pick the fruit, although I know this isn't always possible. Keep the fruit in the fridge for 2 days at the most as it will start to wilt and the pectin levels decrease, making it more difficult to set.

Strawberries are the worst as they start to go mushy really quickly. If you haven't got the time to make the jam, freeze the fruit. Rinse it, weigh the quantity for the recipe plus 10%, lay it on a tray to dry on the windowsill, then label and freeze it. Or make a conserve, which only takes 20 minutes of your immediate time.

For wild fruit don't go picking on main roads where it's most polluted, and don't pick too low down the bush, certainly not at

THE JAMMY BODGER

doggy wee height. It's not always the first thing on your mind, but it is an important consideration!

How much Fruit?

It depends on the size of your jam pan and the number of jars too, but don't use less than 450g (1lb) of fruit, otherwise it's likely to burn on the bottom of the pan, and anyway, it's not worth the effort as you'd only get 1 or 2 jars. If you have a standard jam pan, about 1kg (2lb 4oz) is best, although you can use up to 1.8kg (4lb). Use any more and it will be difficult to set.

Making Pectin Stock

You can make pectin stock with cooking apples, redcurrants or gooseberries, or a mixture of all three. Luckily pectin stock keeps for 4 weeks in the fridge (if Steve doesn't keep opening it thinking it's a jam), or up to 4 months in the freezer in sterilised containers. Remember to leave enough space for expansion, leaving at least 2.5cm / 1inch of your container empty. Like all fruit its pectin level decreases if frozen, so you'd need to add 10% more to any recipe.

Ingredients

750g / 6⅔ cups redcurrants, OR gooseberries (5 cups) OR cooking apples (6 cups chopped)

450ml / 1⅞ cups water

Simmer the fruit and water in the jam pan until completely squishy. Squashing it with the back of the spoon helps.

Meanwhile, place the jelly bag in a small bowl and pour over boiling water from the kettle. Leave the jelly bag in the water until cool, then wring it out and hang it from the jelly stand over the bowl. Leave for a couple of minutes, then wipe up the drips (making sure your cloth is clean and doesn't leave any fibres in the bowl).

Place a pan-stand beside the jelly bag stand, move the jam pan to it and ladle the fruit into the jelly bag, leaving it to drip through.

Whilst it is dripping through, sterilise your jars in the oven and the lids in boiling water as before. Apple and gooseberries seem to take longer to drip through than redcurrants, so wait until it's dripping only once every couple of minutes before sterilising.

Ladle the pectin stock into the jars.

JUNE

Notes from a local producer

Regula Wright, aka Regula Guru, grows all sorts of fruit and veg at The Vege Place, a 2 acre plot of land. Steve helps out, and I use any leftover veg, anything not too pretty or which there's just too much of, but still with tons of flavour, for making jams and chutneys. Over to you, Regula...

I'm not sure where my love of gardening, growing, and harvesting fruit and vegetables came from. Obviously growing up in Switzerland with a large garden with plum, walnut, and cherry trees, as well as a fruit and vegetable plot where we grew all types of salads, tomatoes, and beans, helped. But we were by no means rural as we lived on the edge of a large town, but it was just in the garden and in our food that we kept to traditional ways. I will never forgive my parents for having brown tannin stains on my hands for weeks from peeling walnuts after the early snow before they were ripe, although I still love walnuts now.

Maybe gardening and growing has always been in the back of my mind. I mean it must have been as I studied plant biology and the healing properties of herbs at college, and then started growing my own crops on an allotment 11 years ago. My first crops were the usual potatoes, carrots, beans and spinach, but one real surprise was globe artichokes, which grow really well in a clay soil.

Another motivator is that it's surprisingly tricky to get hold of any tasty fresh vegetables here, so there's a core of like-minded people and businesses who support me, including my new landlord who shares my enthusiasm and ideals. I sell my veg through various local shops, pubs and restaurants, and through a veg box scheme.

Looking ahead to next year I'd like to introduce Indian runner ducks as our pest control squad. On our 2 acre plot we are also going to be growing the normal outdoor stuff from broad beans to pumpkins, plus a good range of salad crops, including all the Japanese leaves and celeriac and fennel which I can't buy anywhere here. The polytunnel will be filled to bursting with Mediterranean plants such as aubergines, peppers and chillies, and also used to prolong the seasons.

I'd like to create a diverse plot where everything works together in balance and rhythm. We input our energy and time, and the soil gives us the crops, and we give back to the soil through compost, seaweed and manure. All the veg is interspersed with perennial and annual flowers to attract pollinating insects, and to give us pleasure. Everyone contributes, even my dog Jim with his ratting, and the chickens and ducks with their eggs and slug and snail eating.

With the rhythm comes a glut of certain vegetables. Our customers can only eat so many courgettes, and marrows are never a favourite, but this glut creates a good, flavourful bounty for making chutneys and jams. I've also planted fruit bushes to support Mel in this, so as well as spray free veg, we have spray free berries, apart from strawberries which the birds have. Plus Mel's favourite, the huckleberries.

Forget Jam – what about Elderflower Cordial?

I've been waiting for elderflowers to make gooseberry and elderflower jam, but the gooseberries aren't playing ball and aren't ripe yet. The elderflower err... tree / bush (I think it's both) is everywhere. You can identify them from their look and smell - they apparently smell like cat's pee. There is a similar looking flower, but it is a much smaller plant with a sturdy stem, so sniff before you pick.

Each flower head contains many tiny little flowers coated in zingy pollen. Resist the urge to pick them all, as both you and the birdies want some of their subsequent berries later in the year.

This year it's mass production as the cordial tastes great, is slightly addictive and pretty expensive in the shops. I've even pre-ordered citric acid from the chemist just in case there is a sudden run on it (like a run on the banks, but maybe not so devastating to the economy), and I've 3 packs of muslin from the hardware store.

Elderflower Cordial

So we pick **10 elderflower heads** from a bush high enough to be safe from doggy wee, pick off any bugs, bag the heads and head for home.

Add **1kg / 5 cups sugar** to a large mixing bowl and pour on **750ml / 3 cups boiling water** and stir to completely dissolve.

Slice **1 lemon finely** and add to the bowl with **25g / 1½ tbsp citric acid,** stir, then submerge the flower heads. Leave them to marinate for **24 hours,** stirring every now and then.

Wash and drain bottles and lids, then rinse in really hot water.

Strain the juice through a sieve **lined with muslin** and pour into the bottles.

Store the cordial in a dark cupboard, and once opened keep in the fridge or freeze in old plastic milk bottles (only filled ¾ full to leave space for expansion), or in ice cube trays.

They make a drink whose flavour I can only compare to a lemon cordial, but with a more subtle hit.

However cautious you are, the occasional batch will contain **bacteria,** shown by cloudy floating bits. Unfortunately it will need to go in the bin. This happened to one bottle we kept in a cupboard for a month before using during a very warm period, so we had provided the perfect conditions for bacteria to breed.

Mid June... Let the Jammy Making Commence!

At last! I've been talking about what I'm going to make, cleaned all the jars people have given me and bought bags and bags of granulated sugar - in short, I'm desperate to get started.

At The Vege Place (see Regula Wright - page 48) the deer have completely outwitted us and snacked on the strawberry plants, whilst we waited for pollination before netting them. Even now 007 Bond-like birdies are going under, over and through anything to get at the few remaining berries; they know they taste good. We have to release them quickly from the netting when they get stuck, otherwise it will be Jim the dog snacking on them.

Luckily the local-ish PYO has got loads of varieties of strawberries and gooseberries and even recommend certain varieties for jam making. I'm hoping the PYO looks after its fruit without too many sprays, as they also sell home-grown meat and vegetables, so I'm assuming they have a decent ethos. I know I should look into this, but am putting it off for now in the rush to make jam.

JAMMY TIP

A full PYO punnet of gooseberries is about a kilo, and a punnet of strawberries will be just under. Pick a bit more than you need so you can eat some and discard any that get squished. The same goes for fruit from the supermarket.

Strawberry & Gooseberry Jam

	Ingredients
No. of jars: 4 medium jars, about 1.3 kg. I lost a bit with scum skimming	450g / 2¼ cups gooseberries
Time taken: Just over an hour	450g / 2¼ cups strawberries
As this jam sets quickly make sure to get your jam jars in the oven early on	3 tbsp water
	900g / 4½ cups sugar

How to Make

Prepare your jars (cold oven 110°C / 225°F / Mk ¼ for 30 minutes) and lids, ladle and funnel (saucepan with boiling water for 20 seconds). Place 3 saucers in the fridge to test for set.

Weigh, then top and tail the gooseberries, scratching off the knobbly bit at one end and pulling out the dark bit of stalk at the other. If you haven't enough nail, use a small knife.

Rinse the gooseberries in a colander, shake to drain, then place in the jam pan with 3 tbsp water.

Simmer the gooseberries gently until their skins soften, stirring occasionally if they are sticking.

Weigh the strawberries, pull off their green tops, rinse, and if they are large, slice them in half.

Once the gooseberries have softened, add the strawberries and simmer for a few minutes until they too start to soften.

Weigh, then add the sugar, stirring continuously until completely dissolved. Scrape the wooden spoon up the side of the jam pan to see if any crystals remain. Stir a bit more to make sure.

Increase the heat and remove the spoon. You are now looking to set the jam.

When the jam is boiling all over the surface (see How To Make Jam, if unsure), take the jam pan off the heat.

Test for set.

When you are happy with the set, skim off the scum.

Give the jam a stir to re-disperse the fruit.

When all the jars are full, twist the lids on tightly and place on a cake rack until cold.

Wipe the jars down, label them and store in a dark place.

Congratulate yourself! The first jam you make is always the hardest!!

Taste Test: It tastes great, without the over sickly sweet taste of plain strawberry, and you never see this in the shops, so it's really a bit special.

Strawberry Jam

Strawberry and gooseberry jam is an easier first jam, as gooseberries are high in pectin, which strawberries lack, so strawberry jam can be a pain to set. To add pectin to strawberries you can either use jam sugar, a bottle or sachet of pectin, or just add lemon juice. The other reason not to make this your first ever jam is the monumental amount of foamy scum that comes off the fruit. See my jam making section for removing the scum.

Make the jam ASAP after picking the fruit as strawberries go squishy fast and their pectin is reduced as time passes. Oh my god! There's not a minute to lose!

No. of jars: 3 medium jars, about 975g. Next time I make it I'm definitely doubling the recipe	Ingredients
	450g / 3⅛ cups strawberries
Time taken: 1 hour, not including fruit picking	400g / 2 cups granulated sugar
Handy hint: If you're worried about scum, add a knob of butter (about 25g / ¼ stick) just after you've added the sugar	2 tbsp lemon juice

JAMMY TIP

I tried to use a strawberry de-huller, but it was more hassle than it was worth, so I just pulled the green tops off.

How To Make

Prepare your jars (cold oven 110°C / 225°F / Mk ¼ for 30 minutes) and lids, ladle and funnel (saucepan with boiling water for 20 seconds). Place 3 saucers in the fridge to test for set.

Weigh the strawberries, remove any green stalks, rinse, drain and slice any large ones in half, then tip them into the jam pan.

Weigh the sugar and juice the lemon.

Heat the strawberries gently to release as much pectin as possible, being careful that they don't stick to the bottom of the jam pan. If they do, decrease the heat and, if needed, add a little bit of water.

When the jam is gently simmering, stir in the sugar and lemon juice until completely dissolved. When you think it's dissolved, stir and draw the spoon up the side of the jam pan to check for sugar crystals. If you find any, keep stirring.

Remove the spoon and bring the jam to the boil, watching out for a boil which covers the whole surface of the jam pan.

When you are happy the jam is set, remove the pan from the heat, give it a gentle stir in one direction to disperse any foam, then leave it to settle for 30 seconds.

Commence scum skimming by scraping the surface of the jam with a tbsp. Don't rush – you will regret it if you just try and stir it in. (I did!)

When all the scum has gone, give the jam a gentle stir and then ladle it through the funnel into the jars.

Twist the lids on tightly, then place the jars on a cake rack to cool. When cold, label and store in a dark place.

Strawberry Conserve

I'm hoping this will be a fruitier adult alternative to the usual strawberry jam. This recipe is great to make if you haven't actually got time to make strawberry jam, as the first step takes about 15 minutes, then you don't do anything until the following day.

No. of jars: 6 medium jars, about 1.9kg Time taken: 2hrs over several days	Ingredients
	1.5kg / 10½ cups strawberries
	1.5 kg / 7½ cups granulated sugar

You need to make space to fit a large bowl in the fridge and some cling film or something to cover it.

There is no testing for set, as conserves have a softer set. You want it thick and gloopy, nearly as thick as you would eat it, as it will thicken more as it sets.

A spatula is your best friend as it makes it easier to scrape sugary gloop from bowl to pan.

How to Make

Stage 1 – no cooking

Weigh, remove any green stalks, then rinse and drain the strawberries in a colander.

Weigh the sugar.

Put some of the strawberries in a large mixing bowl, then some of the sugar, continuing until you are out of both. Then gently fold the mixture with a large spoon until reasonably mixed.

Cover with cling film or a plate and leave to sit for at least 12 hours or overnight.

THE JAMMY BODGER

Stage 2 – warming and short boil

Pour the strawberries into the jam pan and heat gently, stirring gently until all the sugar has dissolved. You can taste the juice left in the bowl as it needs to be washed before the strawberries go back into it anyway. Mmmm... this is going to be good.

Increase the heat and boil steadily, but not like an explosion, for 5 minutes.

Leave to cool, return to the now clean bowl, cover and put back in the fridge for 2 more days.

2 more days pass (this now feels like a film epic!).

Stage 3 – get out your jam making equipment and prepare to boil and pot

Prepare your jars (cold oven 110°C / 225°F/ Mk ¼ for 30 minutes) and lids, ladle and funnel (saucepan with boiling water for 20 seconds). Place 3 saucers in the fridge to test for set.

Pour the strawberries into the jam pan and heat, then boil steadily for about 10 minutes. You aren't boiling as hard as for jam as you are still trying to keep the strawberries in chunks.

After 10 minutes take the jam pan off the heat and check to see if it drips off the spoon in jellified lumps like a not quite set jam, or a thick cheese sauce, but not like water, in which case it has set. If it is still watery, heat at a steady boil for 1 or 2 more minutes, then remove from the heat. You don't want to cook it any more as it will ruin the texture.

Stir gently in one direction to disperse the foam, then attack the scum. Using a tablespoon skim the scum towards the sides of the jam pan and then scrape up and out into a bowl or the saucepan of water.

Leave it to sit for 15 minutes, then stir gently again to disperse the fruit evenly.

Ladle the jam into the jars, then twist the lids on tightly.

Clean the jam pan or leave it to soak, and when the jam is cold, label and store for up to 6 months.

Taste Test: Still very sweet, but now with the whole strawberries it looks really posh. It's got a looser set, so it could be used for a sauce over vanilla ice cream, as a cheesecake topping or to show off by filling a tart case and telling everyone you've spent days slaving over a hot stove. Maybe this is the future of jam making – very little cooking, just lots of stewing.

Blackcurrant Jam

Steve and I picked £29 worth of gooseberries and blackcurrants in the rain; I'm going off jammy action a little at this point. We've got to use the fruit straight away as if you pick damp fruit you can end up with a mouldy jam; but what can you do; it wasn't raining when we arrived at the PYO and we don't want to sit in the coffee shop all day waiting. We'd planned to pick extra fruit for the freezer as both blackcurrants and gooseberries freeze well, but the rain put a stop to that plan.

The 3.5kg of blackcurrants plus water fitted into my large jam pan, but there wasn't enough space for a rapid boil, so I ladled some off into my stock pot and brought both pans to setting point (or so I thought). I made 26 jars of runny, unset jam. If I'm honest I'm still not completely sure what setting point looks like, because the jam (if you can call it that) had been boiling viciously for about 45 minutes. I tested it with the thermometer (pointless) and the saucer, although I admit it was a bit runny on the saucer.

I don't want to have to reset the jam and don't even know how, and to make matters worse I've still got gooseberry and elderflower jam to make. I had to clean the jam pan and start topping and tailing gooseberries as Steve had been back out in the drizzle picking elderflowers, and I didn't have the heart to say I'm not making it now. As the kitchen is out of action (meaning fish and chips for dinner), at least Steve is pleased.

Most Internet recipes for resetting jam use American measurements, but whats a quart?? Eventually I work out that I need to reboil the jam in batches of 4 or 5 jars worth, with the juice of 1 small lemon in each batch. Resetting worked and it made 15 jars, but took about 5 hours to complete, and heaven knows how much electricity, so it's a mistake I hope never to make again.

Fruity Lessons Learnt

From now on I'm going to use under 2kg of fruit.

What the 'I'm setting' boil actually looks like - sometimes the jam pan is too hot in the middle, but the heat hasn't really dispersed enough for setting, so the jam could be throwing out missiles like a volcano, but it's still not set. It needs to do a rolling boil that extends from the middle of the jam pan to the rim.

Making Blackcurrant Jam # 2

I panicked when I opened the oven to sterilise the jars and realised I hadn't cleared up the remnants of a chocolate cake explosion. The shelves and floor of the oven had massive lumps of cake stuck to them. No time now, I reasoned, and tried to ignore the smell of burnt chocolate. The jars appeared unaffected, but if anyone says the jam has a funny flavour I will be horrified.

	Ingredients
No. of jars: 6 medium jars, about 2kg	700g / 6¼ cups blackcurrants
Time taken: 1 hour as it took me ages picking over the fruit as they all had little stalks, which probably would melt away, and I also seemed to have picked a lot of leaves	700g / 3½ cups granulated sugar
	500ml / 2⅛ cups water
If you want a firmer set, reduce the water slightly	

How To Make

Prepare your jars (cold oven 110°C /225°F / Mk ¼ for 30 minutes) and lids, ladle and funnel (saucepan with boiling water for 20 seconds). Place 3 saucers in the fridge to test for set.

Weigh the fruit, then rinse in a colander and pick over, removing any stalks and leaves. This is easier to do in about 3 separate rinses and if you wipe the stalks off your fingers into a small bowl.

Place the fruit in the jam pan with the water and simmer gently until the skins are soft, but the fruit has not completely disintegrated.

When the fruit has softened, reduce the heat and stir in the weighed sugar. Stir until completely dissolved and then increase the heat and look to set the jam.

When the jam is boiling hard and makes a 'put, put, put' sound and when the bubbles burst, take the jam pan off the heat and test for set.

When you are happy with the set, skim off the scum, stir to distribute the fruit, ladle into the jars and twist the lids on tightly.

Taste Test: Definitely a favourite! It's tart and tangy, not sweet and claggy, naming no names.

Variation: Karma Colin makes blackcurrant jam with half the sugar replaced by apples and it's also got the fab twang. His jam won't keep long, but you're probably going it eat it straight away anyway. I stirred some of it into a nearly set cheesecake which was lacking flavour. It went a strange pink, but the flavour was great.

Blackcurrant & Apple Snow

In my first attempt the berries were so sharp it felt like they were stripping the enamel from my teeth, so I've tried to make it less aggressive but still fruity.

Preheat the oven to 200°C / 400°F / Mk 6.

Peel, core and slice **5 eating or 2 cooking apples** and simmer with **50g / ¼ cup sugar**, a squeeze of **lemon juice** and a couple of tablespoons of water until softened. Place in an oven proof dish and stir in **100g / 1 cup blackcurrants**. Whisk **2 egg whites** until they form soft peaks, sprinkle over **50g / ¼ cup caster (superfine) sugar** and continue whisking until the mixture forms stiff peaks. Dollop over the fruit and cook for **20 minutes** or until golden on top.

Gooseberry & Elderflower Jam

The colour of the jam can be anything from pale pink to dark green, depending on your type of gooseberries and whether they are ripe or slightly under ripe.

	Ingredients
No. of jars: 5 small jars, about 1.2kg	900g / 6 cups gooseberries
Time taken: 2 hours	570ml / 2½ cup water
Handy hint: I made this again in July with just 450g fruit. I didn't realise until after I'd potted the jam that I'd burnt the bottom of the jam pan. It didn't affect the flavour, possibly as it wasn't completely blackened, but to stop this happening stir often, and if you need to, add a little more water	900g / 4½ cups sugar
	4 or 5 large elderflower heads (Not got any? That's a shame, but just leave them out)

How to Make

Prepare your jars (cold oven 110°C / 225°F/ Mk ¼ for 30 minutes) and lids, ladle and funnel (saucepan with boiling water for 20 seconds). Place 3 saucers in the fridge to test for set.

Weigh, top and tail, then rinse the gooseberries and place them in the jam pan with the water.

Weigh the sugar.

Bring the gooseberries slowly to a light boil then simmer gently until their skins are completely softened.

Add the sugar and stir constantly until dissolved.

Check for sugar crystals by scraping the spoon up the side of the pan. If any remain there, keep stirring.

Now the sugar has dissolved, hold the elderflower head by the stalk and brush off the flowers into the jam pan with your fingers, trying to keep any stalky bits out.

Heat at full whack until the jam is boiling all over the surface.

The jam is close to setting when you turn your wooden spoon on one side and the jam drips slowly in jellified lumps rather than pouring off like water.

Test for set.

When you're happy the jam is set, remove the jam pan from the heat, stir gently, wait a minute for the jam to settle, then skim off any scum.

Ladle the jam into the jars, twist the lids on tightly and place on a cake rack to cool.

Taste Test: Hooray! This is not a scummy jam and it has a fab, not too sweet flavour with a little tang (I'm told) of Muscat, although I don't know what that or they taste like – well I do now, it tastes like gooseberry and elderflower jam. I am going to make loads of this next year. Diana in the Deli loved it and it's definitely got potential for selling in her shop. I even managed to get a friend addicted to it in a positive way.

Variations: If your gooseberries are tart and you prefer a sweeter jam, add up to another 100g / ½ cup of sugar; you will need to heat another small jar as you will make more jam.

Fruity Lessons Learnt / Things to Ponder

Always carry a plastic bag with you so you can nab some elderflower heads wherever you see them. (I mean when going on a walk, not for when going to business meetings in the middle of a city). I started remembering this after picking some fresh garlic and forgetting I had put it straight into a rucksack - we could never get the smell out.

Get in there first! A friend is getting the empty elderflower cordial bottles from a local coffee shop. They are the perfect size and will look great for gifts.

It's good to check out different PYOs as they will have different varieties of the same crop which are ready at different times, and you can compare prices. Also, some PYOs only really specialise in one fruit, so you may have to go further afield, pick more and freeze some.

I'm really thinking about buying my jars now as sometimes it taking ages to sort the recycled jars out, especially getting the sticky labels off. That's before I even start to clean the kitchen, collect the fruit and then, and only then, make the jam (which sometimes doesn't set!!!!! No, I haven't got over it yet).

If you are knackered when you've finished making jam and don't want to clean the jam pan, just empty the water from the saucepan used for sterilising the lids into the jam pan, plus a couple of kettle loads of hot or cold water and, if you have it, sprinkle some bicarbonate of soda on. Hopefully the cleaning fairies will clean it later, even if that's you, but at least the jam remnants won't have become rock hard. If you need the jam pan immediately, rub some bicarbonate of soda along where the jam boiling line was and then clean with really hot water.

Notes from a local jam maker

Hi! My name is Karma Col and I live in my Karma Cabin and camper van with Pugsley my fat ginger cat and any other animal that turns up. I've spent years travelling around in my camper van and sailing boat, and still take off at the drop of a hat when the mood takes me.

I always come home at some point to face three foot high grass as my garden has run wild. It's a difficult balance between travelling and keeping a veg patch. This summer my garden was really productive. I had blackcurrants, blueberries, and redcurrants planted by my granddad, raspberry, strawberry and incredibly sweet apples from my infamous apple tree, which bears copious amounts of pinky apples every year.

This year I planted goji berries and honey berries (I don't know what they are – I was just given the plants), and harvested tomatoes, potatoes, courgettes, and red cabbage, and have my brothers larger veg patch and Regula as a back up. I'm interested in making my own honey and having chickens.

I've made jam for years. Ever since I was a kid I've always been interested in wild food and living off the land, and I've lived a life away from the system and as much as possible from money. I believe in sharing and trading.

Every year I pick a lot of wild berries because I spend a lot of time travelling, and jam is always handy to take with you. When I make jam it's just out of my head, and its a bit different each time. Honey is a fantastic healer, and I use it a lot in cooking and try to substitute it for sugar wherever possible.

Karma Col's Foraged Berries Jam

1.3kg raspberries 1kg blackcurrants 250g sugar ½ kitchen cup apple juice 1 orange (juice and zest) 500g light honey	Rinse and place the berries, orange zest and juice and apple juice into the jam pan with just enough water to enable the berries to simmer. Reduce the heat and cook until the berries are soft. Add the honey and sugar, increase the heat and look to set.

This set well and we all ate it really quickly, so I couldn't tell you how long it will last, but it won't be too long as it's not got that much sugar. I don't really care if jam making goes wrong. If some don't set I use them as drinks and in natural yoghurt, mix them with porridge or have them on toast.

JULY

There are strawberries, raspberries, blueberries, gooseberries, red, white and blackcurrants and early blackberries ready at the local PYO, although I can't see why you'd pay for blackberries when the free wild ones on the bushes will be ready soon.

It's a good time to remind yourself where free fruits are, and keep an eye on them. I'm watching figs - if they overhang from someone's garden wall I assume they're mine, greengages on common ground, so no dispute there, and the elder bushes everywhere to make sure I catch the berries before the birdies. There are a few wild cherry trees, but the cherries are very small and the birds have already had most of them. I sound like I hate birds, but I really do like them. I just wish they would share nicely.

Gooseberry & Mint Jelly

At last I've got tart gooseberries from The Vege Place and I'm not afraid to use them. I used apple cyder (that's how it's spelt on the bottle) vinegar, as I think malt vinegar will be too harsh and overwhelm all the other flavours. You could use white wine vinegar or any clear vinegar. Darker vinegars would give a funny colour and wouldn't show the mint. My mint rose to the top of each jar after potting, so as the jelly gradually thickened as it cooled, I shook the jars vigorously to disperse the mint. To avoid this, let the jelly thicken enough in the jam pan so it holds the mint before potting.

No. of jars: 5 small jars, so about 1.2kg yield	Ingredients
Time taken: 2 hours, not including drip through time	900g / 6 cups tart gooseberries
Handy hint: As jellies are made in two stages they can either be made over 2 days, or you can just wait a couple of hours for the jelly to drip through the jelly bag, then complete Stage 2	420ml / 1¾ cups water
	420ml / 1¾ cups white vinegar
	600–800g / 3-4 cups granulated sugar
	A bunch of mint
I used golden granulated sugar, but white sugar would be better	3 tbsp fresh, finely chopped mint

Calculating Sugar Formula: 600ml / 2½ cups juice = 450g / 2¼ cups sugar

How to Make

Stage 1

Weigh the gooseberries, top and tail them, rinse in a colander, then tip into the jam pan with the water and un-chopped mint (remembering to keep some mint back for later) and simmer until really soft and squishy.

Boil the kettle, place the jelly bag in a small clean bowl and pour the boiling water over it. Leave it to soak until the water is nearly cold. This is called scalding the jelly bag.

Fit the jelly bag and stand over the bowl.

Once the gooseberries are softened, take the jam pan off the heat and ladle into the jelly bag, being careful not to let any splash straight into the bowl.

Leave the jelly bag to drip through for a couple of hours or overnight.

Don't squish or squeeze the fruit in the jelly bag as you will end up with a cloudy jelly.

Stage 2 – setting the jelly

Prepare your jars (cold oven 110°C / 225°F / Mk ¼ for 30 minutes) and lids, ladle and funnel (saucepan with boiling water for 20 seconds). Place 3 saucers in the fridge to test for set.

Once the jelly bag is no longer dripping, carry the whole stand carefully (minus the bowl filled with juice) to the sink in case of spillage, remove the jelly bag from the stand and empty the jelly bag contents either into the bin or compost caddy. Rinse the jelly bag and place it in a bowl of hot water to clean later.

Pour or ladle the jelly juice from the bowl into a measuring jug. Note the amount, then pour the juice into the jam pan.

Warm the jam pan gently and finely chop your mint.

Work out the amount of sugar to add using the Calculating Sugar Formula beneath the Ingredients and add to the jam pan.

Stir continuously until all the sugar has dissolved, then whack the heat to high and start looking to set the jelly. When the jelly is boiling all over the surface and when the bubbles burst they make a 'put,put, put' sound, take the jam pan off the heat and start testing for set.

When you are happy with the set, stir the jelly gently to disperse any foam, then skim off any scum.

Sprinkle in the finely chopped mint and stir gently.

Leave the jam pan to rest for about 10 minutes so that the jelly thickens slightly, then stir again to disperse the mint evenly.

Ladle into the jars, twist the lids on tightly and when cool wipe, label and store.

Taste Test: Fish Shop Julia says this goes great with lamb as it cuts through the fatty juices. I'm hoping it will go with mackerel, but Julia's not eaten fish this week (better not tell the customers!). I think it's possibly too vinegary, but I am going to wait a couple of weeks and then try again.

Taste Test 2: Ooh! Surprisingly good. Just the right amount of tart, tangy mintiness to go with my lamb chops tonight.

Gooseberry Curd

I'd like to make a tart, tingling curd which can compete with lemon curd, but I'm not sure how much butter, sugar or eggs to add. I spent ages reading recipes, only to conclude it's pretty much down to individual taste.

How did I work out how long this curd keeps for? I kept 2 jars in a cool, dark cupboard and after 3 months it still tasted great. After 4 months it had separated with a thin layer of water at the bottom, so nobody fancied eating it. Curd is best enjoyed when made. Don't worry if it's a little too thin, or if you want to really decrease the sugar just keep the curd in the fridge. For further info on making curds see the section on making curds.

No. of jars: 7 small jars, yielding about 1.7kg (you can halve this recipe)	**Ingredients**
Time taken: 2 hours not including the hour I spent at the shops when I realised the ceramic mixing bowl had a crack in the bottom	900g / 6 cups gooseberries
	100ml / ½ cup (just under) water
	115g / ½ cup (1 stick) unsalted butter
Handy hint: If the curd is still struggling to set say 20 minutes after adding the egg, check that the water is simmering fast enough, and if it is add an extra egg yolk or 2	300g / 1½ cups granulated or caster sugar
	4 eggs

This curd will keep for approximately 3 months in a cool, dark cupboard, although it prefers the fridge.

How To Make

Weigh, top and scratch the tails, then rinse the gooseberries in a colander.

Simmer the gooseberries and water in a saucepan until the fruit is completely squishy. If the fruit threatens to stick, add another tablespoon of water.

Prepare your jars (cold oven 110°C / 225°F / Mk ¼ for 30 minutes) and lids, ladle and funnel (saucepan with boiling water for 20 seconds). Place 3 saucers in the fridge to test for set.

Ladle the gooseberry juice into a sieve held above a large bowl and press through the fruity juice with the back of a spoon, one or two ladles at a time. Don't forget to scrape the back of the sieve. This takes a while.

Wipe clean the large saucepan and wash and drain the sieve.

Place the bowl of gooseberries above the large saucepan filled with 2 or 3cm of water (bain marie style). The bowl's base must not touch the water.

Bring the water to a fast simmer and try not to let it boil, as water will evaporate up the sides of the bowl and if the bowl gets too hot when the egg is added, it will curdle.

Add the butter and sugar to the gooseberries in the bowl (BUT NOT THE EGGS YET!). Stir occasionally with a spatula or wooden spoon until the butter and sugar have dissolved.

Whisk the eggs in a small bowl, take the gooseberries and the saucepan off the heat and sieve in the eggs. Rub the eggs through the sieve with a spoon and scrape the bottom of the sieve to remove any egg that is clinging on.

Return the gooseberry curd to the heat and stir or whisk occasionally until thick, then stir continuously, particularly scraping around the edge of the bowl.

When the curd is thick and coats the back of the wooden spoon (this will take some time, so be patient), it is done. It needs to be nearly at eating thickness. It will thicken further in the jar, but only slightly.

Take the bowl off the saucepan and ladle the curd into the warm jars.

Twist the lids on tightly and place on a cake rack to cool.

Wait for the curd in the bowl to cool slightly, then use your fingers to clean.

The curd should keep for a couple of months in a cool cupboard, but must be kept in the fridge and used within 4 weeks of opening.

Mmm... stirring the curd into custard, then leaving it in the fridge for a bit, makes a quick gooseberry fool.

Seasonal recipes / leftover berries: I reheated the gross coloured gooseberry pulp that didn't go through the sieve with a bit of water. I was originally going to use it to top a cheesecake, always a favourite, but decided it was too pippy and put a crumble topping on it, reasoning that as it was cooked again the seeds would soften, and they did seem to.

Gooseberry Crumble

Layer the gooseberry sludge on the bottom of an oven proof dish. You could add elderflowers if you wish. Rub **60g butter / ¼ cup (½ stick)** into **120g / 1 cup self raising flour** (if you haven't got any, use plain) together to form bread crumbs and mix in **2 tbsp sugar**. Top the goosie sludge with the crumble, then sprinkle more **sugar** on top. Cook in the oven on high for about 20 minutes or until the crumble is crunchy. This crumble can top any leftover berries or apples and the tarter the better. You can also mix ground almonds into the crumble and top with brown sugar, if you prefer.

Gooseberry & Lemon Cheesecake

Cheesecake	Berry topping
200g / 2 cups crushed ginger biscuits or digestives (about 20 2" diameter biscuits)	200g-ish / 1½ cups berries (or whatever you've got to hand)
100g / ⅞ stick butter, melted	
500g / 2¼ cups soft cream cheese (no herbs or garlic!)	
50g / ½ cup sieved icing / powdered sugar	
The finely grated zest and juice of 2 lemons	

Mix the crushed biscuits and melted butter, press into the base of a 7 inch / 18cm cake tin or similar sized container and chill whilst you continue.

Beat together the rest of the ingredients, pour on top of the biscuit base and chill for 1 hour in the fridge.

Simmer the berries gently – you are only warming them. If they are too tart, add a little sugar. When the berries are cool and when the cheesecake comes out of the fridge, pour the berries on top and keep in the fridge until needed.

You can use limes, oranges or any citrus fruit in place of the lemons. The cheesecake will not set completely firm and will have a slight wibble wobble; most that set really firm use gelatine and I'm not a fan of piggy bits in my cheesecake, although I'd like to try agar flakes at some point, although that's adding algae, so that's a bit strange too.

Lemon curd cheesecake – you can make the cheesecake, leave it to thicken slightly, then swirl some lemon curd through it.

Or my own favourite, which I make far too often; a really zesty lemon cheesecake.

Pick and Freeze

I picked about 1kg of gooseberries and rinsed, weighed and popped them in the freezer in a container with the weight noted on it. I feel very efficient. Thou shalt have gooseberry jam outside of summer. (See Freezing in the FAQs)

If you don't want to add a berry topping, add more zest to the cheesecake, but not more juice as that makes it too liquidy.

Blueberry & Lime Jam

I'm approaching this recipe with an open mind. Yes I know blueberries are a super food, but I have always found them bland and tasteless. At least I like lime. We picked the blueberries at a small PYO that specialises in them. I wondered why there weren't many weeds; no, I couldn't just enjoy myself, so I asked what the blueberries are sprayed with. The couple who run the place (smallholders?? farmers??) explained that the ground is sprayed, not the bushes. I really want to use them so I think I should research what I am asking so I can be more specific. Blueberries aren't native to Britain, which might mean they need loads of spray to keep them healthy, which could be why they are expensive. Blueberries cost £5.99 a kilo compared

THE JAMMY BODGER

Let the conserve rest in the jam pan for about 10 minutes after it has set so that the conserve thickens slightly, then stir to distribute the fruit, unless of course you want all your fruit to float to the top in the jars; Diana in the Deli was very impressed with my top floating fruit, so I didn't like to admit it was a mistake.

No. of jars: 7 small jars approximately, yielding about 1.8kg	Ingredients
	900g / 6½ cups cherries (with stones / pits)
Conserves look best in small or tall and thin jars, as they looks posh	750g / 3¾ cups granulated sugar
	2 juiced lemons
Time taken: 1½ hours, plus standing time	1 pectin sachet or ½ bottle liquid pectin (you don't need to add more lemon juice or use jam sugar instead of granulated)

How To Make

Stage 1

Weigh then rinse the cherries and place in a colander. De-stone and de-stalk them and place in a large glass bowl, trying not to lose too much juice.

Weigh the sugar and gently stir it into the cherries. Cover the bowl and place in the fridge if it's a warm day, and leave for at least four hours or overnight.

Stage 2

Pour the cherries and sugar (if using a pectin sachet, add now) into the pan, stir gently on a low heat until the sugar has dissolved, then add the lemon juice.

JAMMY TIP

You WILL need a cherry stoner!

Prepare your jars (cold oven 110°C / 225°F / Mk ¼ for 30 minutes) and lids, ladle and funnel (saucepan with boiling water for 20 seconds). Place 3 saucers in the fridge to test for (a rough) set.

Increase the heat in the jam pan until you have a steady boil – not manic as for jam, but bubbling all over the surface of the pan and don't stir. If using bottled pectin remove the jam pan from the heat after 2 minutes of rapid boiling and stir in the pectin, then act as if it has set.

Start testing for set. Remember, you are only looking for a loose set, so when it's dripping jellified-ish on the spoon and staying apart for a short while on the saucer, turn off the heat.

Stir in one direction to disperse any foam, then skim off any scum. There's hardly any scum, but what there is is hard to get off because the fruit seems to hang on as if for dear life. Of course you don't want to lose the fruit, but persevere and get rid of as much as possible.

Leave to stand for 10 minutes for the conserve to thicken slightly. Stir gently to disperse the fruit evenly and ladle into the jars, trying to get about the same amount of fruit and juice in each one.

Place on a cake rack and leave to cool, then label and store in a dark cupboard for up to 6 months, which rules this out for Christmas, which is a shame.

For a more extravagant feel you can stir in a couple of tablespoons of booze like kirsch, brandy, sloe gin or vanilla extract, but only after setting point has been reached, so you don't just boil it straight off.

Golden and green courgettes, beetroot, new carrots, spring onions, new potatoes and so much more... I'm in veg heaven. I really want to be cooking, not jamming, which has kind of taken over.

At The Vege Place three picnic benches are laden with big plastic trays filled with onions, but still the onions aren't drying quickly enough to prevent some going mouldy. So even though summer fruits are still crying out to be picked, it's ALSO chutney time and I'm not sure what to make first!

Caramelised Onion Marmalade

No. of jars: 6 small jars yielding approximately 1.5kg Time taken: About 3 hours, what with all that chopping. Unfortunately I forgot to record	Ingredients
	2kg / 12½ cups chopped large red or brown onions
	350ml / 1½ cups vinegar
	200g / 1 cup (packed) light or dark brown sugar
	150g / ½ cup redcurrant jelly
	15-20 crushed peppercorns, or use a pepper mill to grind a load
	1 or 2 tsp salt to taste
	1 tbsp chilli powder, Cayenne pepper, or paprika to taste
	2 bay leaves
	100ml / ½ cup oil or melted butter

I like the idea of caramelised onion chutney with no raisins to go in a cheese roll, or to stir into a sausage casserole.

THE JAMMY BODGER

It tastes vinegary, so it's hard to work out if the flavour is right. Just add the ingredients you like and wait a few weeks with your fingers crossed.

A large pan with a lid is good for making this, or fry the onions first in a deep frying pan with a lid and then, if there isn't enough space for the liquid, transfer to the jam pan before adding the vinegar.

How to Make

Slice the onions as finely as possible and fry them gently in butter or oil on a low heat with the pan covered, stirring occasionally until the onions are soft and translucent, usually for about 30 minutes.

Add the sugar, bay leaves, redcurrant jelly, chilli powder or other (if using), salt and peppercorns and stir until it is all brown and glossy.

Simmer the uncovered chutney gently to let the flavours infuse, stirring occasionally, for about 30 minutes, until the onions are nearly dry.

Take the onions off the heat and let them cool for a couple of minutes.

Add the vinegar, then bring the chutney to the boil and boil hard for about 10 minutes.

Boil gently in a rapid simmer until all the liquid has evaporated and the chutney is thick and glossy.

JAMMY TIP

The chutney is not done until you can draw a line across the surface and it leaves an indent for a moment, or you draw a line across the bottom of the pan and it stays apart; when it's nearly at a consistency you could imagine eating, and all the surface liquid has evaporated.

Prepare your jars (cold oven 110°C / 225°F / Mk ¼ for 30 minutes) and lids, ladle, funnel and bubble bursting knife (saucepan with boiling water for 20 seconds).

Ladle the chutney into the jars, tapping each jar on the work surface to help the chutney settle. Fill to within 5mm of the top of each jar, just past the shoulders, so that when it settles and shrinks back a little the jar won't look half full.

Use the knife to burst any air bubbles, then gently draw the knife back out of the jar. Make sure to get rid of all large air bubbles and top up the chutney if it's settled too much.

Leave for at least a couple of weeks before tasting.

Taste Test: Great with everything. I've made this again and again and again.

Strawberry Freezer Jam

Quantity: 2 plastic lunch boxes filled ¾ full, so as to leave space	Ingredients
	500g / 3½ cups strawberries at room temperature
	1 tbsp lemon juice
Time taken: 30 minutes	1 tbsp agar flakes or 1 tsp agar powder
	60–115g / ⅓-⅔ cup caster sugar (superfine)

At first I thought 'Why freeze jam when it keeps for ages anyway?' Then I realised that that this type of jam might taste more like fresh fruit because the fruit is uncooked.

Firstly you need to find agar flakes in either a health food shop or a larger supermarket. They are made from algae and are a setting agent, so you don't need to add pectin or boil the jam.

If you can't find these flakes, add half a bottle of liquid pectin and two tbsp of lemon juice.

How To Make

Give the strawberries a quick rinse, take the green stalky bits off and place in a large bowl with the lemon juice.

Crush the berries with a fork. You are aiming for a rough purée, so lumps are fine.

Put 250ml / 1 cup of water into a small saucepan and add the agar flakes. Leave for 2-3 minutes to soften, then give the pan a swirl and bring to the boil over a low heat without stirring.

Simmer gently for 5 minutes, stirring occasionally until all the flakes have dissolved.

Add the sugar and stir occasionally until all the sugar has dissolved (about 3 or 4 minutes).

Pour the syrup onto the fruit, stirring constantly until well mixed.

Pour into a freezer container, leaving a 2cm (¾ in) space at the top for expansion.

Allow the jam to cool, then seal, leave in the fridge overnight, then freeze.

To use, defrost overnight in the fridge, then keep in the fridge and use within 2 weeks.

Taste Test: I didn't try this until September. It's really fresh and vibrant, but mine was just a fruit purée, not a jam. That said, it's great on cereals and really tastes of strawberries, so it's a great way to extend the season.

Pesticides and Fertilisers

After reading an email from the RSPCA about the plight of honey bees, which seem to be disappearing fast, I at last emailed the manager of the local PYO, Holme for Gardens, to ask what insecticides and pesticides (specifically nicotinoids, which have been shown to have a negative impact on bee populations), are sprayed on the fruit bushes and the weeds around them.

Luckily it's all good. The following is an excerpt from an email from Simon Goldsack, owner of Holme for Gardens. Luckily he has kept it in layman's speak, and explains why certain sprays have to be used in order for there to be any fruit left to pick.

"I have a general understanding of what is applied to the crops. We try where possible to avoid chemicals and use cultural control as much as we can. We do, however, have to keep the farm looking tidy so we use weed control in the bush fruit. This is applied in the winter and gives control for most of the season. We also use mulches generated from our own chipped wood and the rest from recycled garden waste from Eco Sustainable Solutions.

Raspberries are prone to botrytis and raspberry beetle. The former cause the fruit to rot and the latter is a white maggot that burrows into the fruit, not nice for customers so we have to treat these.

Strawberries again are prone to botrytis. To control this we go for a wider spacing but if it gets into the crop early or if the season is particularly wet it can be a problem. Organic growers grow them under huge plastic tunnels which are unsightly and we can't do as we are in an area of outstanding natural beauty.

With most of the bush fruit the main problems are powdery mildew but we hardly spray for this because we have selected to grow mildew resistant varieties. So gooseberries, blackcurrants, red and white currants have very little or no spray for mildew. Gooseberries are prone to sawfly larvae, a type of caterpillar which completely denudes the plant of leaf and weakens it for future years. We do use an insecticide on this about 6 weeks before harvest.

Our Fruit Farm Manager has checked and we do not use any nicotinoids in any of the sprays we apply to our crops. If we do have to use an insecticide we spray either after 8pm at night or before 6am to minimise the risk to bees. Bees are essential to us on the fruit farm. No bees - no pollination - no fruit! We have 8 hives on the fruit farm."

Emailing the farm has an added bonus. Simon told me that his wife, Liz, makes about 1000 jars of jam every year, making between 3 and 10 batches each week, and asked if I'd like to meet up with her for a chat.

It was interesting to meet someone already making so much jam, and it's amazing that someone with a family and a business to help run can get that much jam produced. It makes my efforts look trifling. Anyway, information gained: strawberry is a scummy jam (I know, I'm a bit obsessed) and Liz has several inches of scum on each batch, but only 1 batch has ever been ruined by being too cloudy, as most skims off and the rest can be stirred in.

Fruity Lessons to Ponder - I Need to:

Think about making my own pectin stock. I've heard you can add apple peel to boost a low pectin jam, but nothing definite. I think last year's apples are still available from store, but surely you can't make pectin stock from them as their pectin level will have decreased in storage?

Think about ordering lemons in bulk from an organic wholesaler like Somerset Organic Link. Lemons are used in so many jam recipes to top up the pectin or acid levels, but I can't always get hold of organic un-waxed ones, and when I can they are small, a bit shrivelled and cost a lot. Not very satisfying.

Get jars and lids sorted before jam time and don't delay. I spent so long dithering about ordering some that when there was a delay in delivery I lost about 2 weeks of precious jam making time, as although I had jars I didn't have lids as so many of the lids I am given are knackered.

I must order extra lids next time I order jars. You can buy them in packs of 3 or 4 from the hardware store, but it's not ideal when you are making loads.

If using recipes taken from the Internet, either only use ones from well-known foodie sources, or if using a stranger's recipe, compare the quantities of sugar and vinegar with those in jammy books to make sure the chutney will keep.

A friend (I'm naming no names) overcooked a jam as they weren't sure if they had reached setting point or not. The result was a sticky gloop stuck in the jars which resembled the remnants of boiled sweets. The jars had to be warmed to remove the contents, which were then all put back in the jam pan with some more water. Apparently it then set into a pretty decent jam, but this did remind me to take the jam pan off the heat when checking for the setting point.

Notes from a local jam maker

I always thought jam making would take ages and be too difficult, but I've loved it, so just give it a go. Get everything ready first, then it's not stressful and you're not trying to find everything as you remember it. I like to make jam when I'm on my own for the evening with a good selection of music to dance around the kitchen to, willing what's in the pan to set.

What I don't understand is why everything you want to pick is guarded by nettles and brambles? Be prepared and wear protection (of the glove kind!), otherwise your hands and legs will look like you've been attacked by cats. Ian is a reluctant picker and sorter of fruit, and likes to take the credit for all my hard work. My dog, Blue, gets a bit fed up with waiting around while we go picking, but will happily lick any spilt jam off the floor!

I made the mistake once of washing my blackberries and elderberries, then leaving them overnight and they went mouldy, so I won't do that again. Hubby Ian was not amused as we had to go and pick them again.

I sterilise my jars in the oven and lids in boiling water. I always put the jars through the dishwasher first to be sure they're clean. I should really look up how to sterilise in the dishwasher – it must be easier. I find a jam funnel essential, and plenty of clean cloths for clumsy people like me. I like having an egg timer to help with timings, and to keep a record of how long things take so you know roughly how long it will take next time. I test for set using cold side plates in the fridge, and my finger running through it.

As for the foam / scum, I think it tastes great on ice cream. The raspberry foam I froze and used with some fresh fruit on a cheesecake. Also I find nail varnish helps get some of the more stubborn labels off jars.

At the start I didn't really give myself enough time to sort through the fruit, and have spent many a night still making jam at midnight.

My favourite preserve is raspberry, having made the raspberry fridge jam which is a definite winner with me, or anything with gooseberry. Ian's favourite bought jam is wild blueberry, but I haven't found any reasonably priced local blueberries yet.

Of the jams I've made, Ian's favourite was strawberry and raspberry, although he seems to go through a jar a week, whatever it is!

Strawberry & Raspberry Jam

Strawberries and raspberries in equal amounts

Granulated sugar (the same weight as the total fruit)

The juice of 1 lemon per 900g of total of fruit

Simmer the fruit until soft, then add the sugar, stirring until it has dissolved.

Add the lemon juice, increase the heat, and look to set the jam.

This sets much easier and generates less foam than plain strawberry jam. It tastes sweet, but more interesting than the single fruits on their own.

Jen xx

AUGUST

THE JAMMY BODGER

Pick! Pick! Pick! We're off to the PYO. I was planning to pick strawberries and gooseberries, but I'm thwarted as the strawberries have been picked out and the gooseberries have passed their astringent prime and are now perfectly edible, so won't have the sharpness needed for jam.

But hooray! The raspberries are out at last. They are £1 more a punnet, but I think their flavour will be worth the extra pennies. It's strange picking raspberries as they don't look shiny and fresh, but they taste great, so it's just careful picking to avoid any mouldy ones. Pick 250g more raspberries to freeze to make raspberry and blood orange curd, or freeze 500g to make a raspberry curd.

If your PYO has a website then check out what's available before you go picking. Alternatively, when you turn up have a back up plan, and perhaps have a comprehensive jam recipe book with you too. We took the weighing scales with us once, but that wasn't very practical.

Raspberry Fridge Jam

This retains the full flavour of the berry as they aren't cooked, but simply mashed with warm sugar. Use the biggest bowl you've got and stir the sugar in before starting to mash. I pushed my potato masher into the bowl and sugar hit my legs, arms, work surfaces and went all over the floor. Then for some reason I did it again before stopping to get a spoon. After stirring a few times I mashed again with much more success. I was worried the sugar hadn't all dissolved, but as I gave this jam away to 6 different people and they all ate it straight from the jar, I don't think it was a problem.

This would be good to make with kids as there's no boiling fruit. This is one of the few recipes that must be made with the fruit straight after picking or bought fruit that is ripe and in perfect condition.

No. of jars: 7 small jars, yielding about 1.7kg (you get about 200g more than the weight of the fruit)	Ingredients
Time taken: 45 minutes	1240g / 10 cups raspberries 1240g / 6¼ cups caster sugar

How To Make

Weigh then rinse and drain your fruit, leaving it to drain in a colander.

Prepare your jars (cold oven 110°C / 225°F / Mk ¼ for 30 minutes) and lids, ladle and funnel (saucepan with boiling water for 20 seconds). Place 3 saucers in the fridge to test for set.

Weigh out the same amount of sugar as fruit, place in an oven proof dish and put in the oven with the jars for 15-20 minutes.

Check your sugar. I stuck my finger in it, but rather than risk the heat, spoon a little out and then stick your finger in it. It needs to be warm, not hot.

When the sugar is warm, empty the raspberries into a large bowl and pour the sugar on top, stirring gently to combine.

Then mash for all you are worth until there are no grainy bits left – up the sides of the bowl or anywhere else.

Ladle into the jars, twist the lids on and leave on a cake rack to cool – it won't take long.

Label the jars 'Please Keep Me In The Fridge,' and eat within a couple of weeks, or use straight away in a Victoria sandwich cake with butter icing.

Redcurrant Jelly

When I needed redcurrant jelly for caramelised onion marmalade I used shop-bought, which had a slightly slimy texture and that fake fruity taste that makes me shake my head as if I've just tasted a very cheap, dry wine (which after a couple of sips I don't actually mind). So I'm going to see if my own tastes better.

No. of jars: A measly 2½ small jars, yielding about 600g, but it was worth it	Ingredients
Time taken: 1 hour sorting and simmering, then left to drain overnight and 45 minutes the next day	1.24kg / 11 cups redcurrants 200ml / ⅞ cup water 1kg / 5 cups (at the most) granulated sugar

Calculating Sugar Formula: 600ml / 2½ cups juice = 450g / 2¼ cups sugar

How To Make

Stage 1

Weigh, rinse and drain the fruit, and simmer gently with the water in the jam pan until the fruit is completely mulched after about 30-45 minutes.

Set up your jelly bag and stand, scalding the jelly bag first.

Ladle the fruit mulch into the jelly bag and leave to drip through.

Stage 2

Prepare your jars (cold oven 110°C / 225°F / Mk ¼ for 30 minutes) and lids, ladle and funnel (saucepan with boiling water for 20 seconds). Place 3 saucers in the fridge to test for set.

THE JAMMY BODGER

Empty the jelly bag into the bin or compost bin and rinse the jelly bag and place it in a bowl of hot water with a bit of washing up liquid. Leave it to rinse out later.

Pour the juice from the bowl into a measuring jug, then note the amount and pour it into the jam pan. Warm the juice on a low heat.

Use the Calculating Sugar Formula beneath the Ingredients to work out how much sugar to add. I only got 500ml / just over 2 cups of juice, so added 375g / almost 2 cups of sugar.

Add the sugar and stir until completely dissolved, then increase the heat and look to set the jelly. Remember jelly sets quick.

Test for set, definitely taking the jam pan off the heat each time you test.

When you are happy with the set, skim off any scum, then ladle through the funnel into the jars and twist the caps on tightly.

Taste Test: So much better than shop-bought. Bring it out whenever you have a roast or a leftover roast sandwich, or have it with brie or mozzarella.

Don't squish or squeeze the fruit in the jelly bag as you will end up with a cloudy jelly.

Raspberry & Redcurrant Jam

I'm using up fruity leftovers, but ideally use equal quantities of both fruits and the same amount in total of sugar. The raspberries are added later as they are softer and if you simmer them for too long they turn to mush. This jam produced a few big lumps of scum, which were easy to spoon off.

Handy hint: You could sieve the fruit before adding the sugar to get rid of the raspberry pips and treat it as a jelly by adding 450g / 2 cups of sugar to each 600ml / 2 cups of juice. You could also double the quantities of fruit and sugar if you have a large jam pan.

No. of jars: 2 small, 2 medium, and a ½ jar approximately, or about 1.2 kg	Ingredients
	472g / 4¼ cups redcurrants
	428g / 3½ cups raspberries
Time taken: About an hour, but difficult to tell as I was making pectin stock at the same time	5 tbsp water
	900g / 9½ cups granulated sugar

How to Make

Weigh the redcurrants, then rinse and pick over to get rid of any leaves you might have collected.

Place the redcurrants in the jam pan with the water and simmer gently, squishing with the back of the spoon until really soft.

Meanwhile weigh the raspberries, then rinse and pick over to remove any that are knackered (and check the weight again if you've had to discard a lot).

Prepare your jars (cold oven 110°C / 225°F / Mk ¼ for

30 minutes) and lids, ladle and funnel (saucepan with boiling water for 20 seconds). Place 3 saucers in the fridge to test for set.

Add the raspberries and simmer for 5 minutes.

Weigh the sugar, bashing out any lumps in it. I think mine was lumpy from being in the cupboard by the oven.

Reduce the heat, or move the jam pan off the heat, and stir in the sugar. Keep stirring until the sugar has completely dissolved.

Return the jam pan to the stove and increase the heat. Start looking to set the jam.

When you are happy with the set, ladle into the jars and twist the lids on tightly.

Taste Test: Lovely and tart. I think I'm going to have to hide this.

Gooseberry & Elderflower Cordial Jam

You can add the cordial after the sugar and before boiling for a set, or after the jam has set. I used **900g of berries (6 cups)** and **sugar (4½ cups), 150ml / ⅔ cup of water** and **4 tbsp of cordial**, which I decided to add after the sugar had dissolved.

Taste Test: Not as great as I had hoped as the goosies are a bit long in the tooth. The jam is now pippy like raspberry jam, and the cordial gives a stronger flavour rather than the more effervescent (I think that's the right word) elderflowers. I'd use cordial again, but with goosies at their tart best.

More Fruity Action

I got 12 nectarines from the market for the bargain price of £3. I've now added nectarines to the In Season Guide, although I'm not sure where they are in season; possibly not here as I've never seen a nectarine tree. Nectarines have to be prepped a bit like red tomatoes to get the skin off, and then if you want to you can bash the stone and remove the kernel within, adding the kernel to the jam pan for extra flavour.

I'm going to wait until the end of cooking and then see if the jam could benefit from the vanilla treatment, or maybe a slug of brandy. I'm not sure what fruit goes with which flavourings, but I think I need to stock up in the Christmas sales on some of the weird fruity brandies and liqueurs. Many online recipes seem to recommend adding candied ginger, cinnamon sticks or vanilla sugar.

Nectarine & Brandy Jam

No. of jars: 5 large jars, yielding approximately 2.25kg	Ingredients
	1.2kg / 7-9 medium nectarines or peaches
Time taken: 1 hour (and that was rushing a bit as I had a train to catch)	1kg / 5 cups sugar
	300ml / 1¼ cups water
	4tbsp lemon juice
	2 tbsp brandy / whisky (optional)

Nectarines are slippery blighters once peeled and you need to chop them into quite small size dice as they take quite a while to simmer down. My chunks were too large, so I had to squish them with the potato masher. If I'd diced them better they could have stayed whole.

Bashing the stone to release the kernel posed a few problems. I didn't want to make too much noise walloping the stones in a plastic bag with the rolling pin as I didn't think my neighbours would appreciate it early in the morning, so I left Steve to deal with it. Unfortunately Steve rose to the challenge a bit too enthusiastically, and when he returned from outside I don't know what he'd done, but the plastic bag was full of shrapnel. If I'd added any it would have been impossible to find and remove them before potting the jam, and would have made eating it like chewing grit. Of course I thanked Steve for his help.

Handy hint: I think the easiest way to remove the kernels from the stones would be in a pestle and mortar, or maybe with a large nut cracker. (Even more special equipment. I'm just getting over the cherry stoner and strawberry huller). Even then you'd have to remember to keep a look out for them so as to remove them before potting the jam.

P.S The lemon juice is added at the start to stop the fruit going a funny colour.

How to Make

Weigh the fruit, then place it in a large bowl and pour boiling water over the top. Leave it for 30 seconds then drain, peel and chop the fruit. Place it in the jam pan with the water and lemon juice.

Bring to the boil and then simmer gently until the fruit has softened.

(If you're feeling motivated bash the stones, remove the kernels and add them to the jam pan, remembering to remove them before potting).

Prepare your jars (cold oven 110°C / 225°F / Mk ¼ for 30 minutes) and lids, ladle and funnel (saucepan with boiling water for 20 seconds). Place 3 saucers in the fridge to test for set.

When the fruit has softened, add the sugar, stirring until dissolved, then increase the heat and look to set the jam.

When you are happy with the set, remove the jam pan from the heat and stir in the brandy. If using the kernels, remember to remove them at this point.

There should be hardly any scum, but give it a quick skim if needed and then pot.

Taste Test: It's completely different to other jams and reminds me of a jam that could be used with custard as a pudding. I can't quite put my finger on it. It's not really a breakfast jam, except maybe on fruit toast or toast later in the day, or in the middle of a cake.

Rowan Berry & Apple Jelly

The Rowan berries are turning from orange to red. As it's been hot and dry I think they are ripening early and although if you taste one they make your stomach turn over in a bad way, apparently they are supposed to taste like this, and their flavour is offset by apples. Although the rowans will be on the tree for another month, I'm worried the birdies are going to get them - sheer madness on their part - so I'm going to pick them quickly.

Handy hint: Start by adding the lesser amount of water. I ended up adding more as my berries were still very solid, and my eating apples needed more water to soften.

JAMMY TIP

Make this jelly after the berries have been out on the tree for a while and have had a chance to sweeten.

No. of jars: 3 small ones, about 700g	Ingredients
	500g / 3⅓ cups rowan berries
Time taken: 11.00am start, a 30 minute simmer, left until 3.00pm to drip through the jelly bag, then another 30 minutes to finish	400g apples (5 small ones)
	1kg / 5 cups granulated sugar (probably nowhere near this, but you never know)
	750ml / 3⅛ cups water (450ml / 1⅞ cups if using cooking apples)
Calculating Sugar Formula: 600ml / 2½ cups juice = 450g / 2¼ cups sugar	

How to Make

Stage 1

Rinse and weigh the berries and add them to the jam pan with the water. Peel, dice and weigh the apples and add them to the jam pan.

Simmer for about 30 minutes until the fruit is very soft, squidging it to a pulp with the back of the spoon.

Scald the jelly bag, then set it up on the stand.

Ladle the fruit pulp into the jelly bag and leave to drip through for three or four hours, overnight, or until it has stopped dripping.

Stage 2

Prepare your jars (cold oven 110°C / 225°F / Mk ¼ for 30 minutes) and lids, ladle and funnel (saucepan with boiling water for 20 seconds). Place 3 saucers in the fridge to test for set.

Pour the fruity juice into a measuring jug and use the sugar formula to work out how much sugar to add.

Pour the fruity juice into the jam pan and when warm stir in the sugar, stirring until it has dissolved. Increase the heat and look to set.

When set, take the jam pan off the heat and scrape off the sum on top of the jelly. Don't try and stir it in.

Ladle into jars and twist the lids on tightly.

Taste Test: Initially so bitter I thought it inedible, but I tried it again a week later and you get sweetness first, then just a slightly bitter aftertaste.

Mediterranean Chutney

Mmm... courgettes, aubergines, peppers. I really fancy a ratatouille-like chutney.

No. of jars: 7½ small jars, about 1.8kg	Ingredients
Time taken: 2½ hours	900g / 5 cups chopped red toms
You need a lid for your pan. I didn't check and was cursing myself as I made this in my large jam pan, which doesn't have one	900g / 6-10 cups chopped peppers, aubergines, courgettes or small marrows all together
	4 cloves garlic, crushed
	800g / 5 cups finely chopped onions
	350g / 1¾ cups granulated sugar
	300ml / 1¼ cups red / white wine / balsamic vinegar
It's difficult to work out how many cups a mixture of vegetables make, therefore unfortunately the cup sizes sound a bit random. I'm sorry. If it helps 900g = 2lb	1 tsp each salt and pepper
	1 tbsp finely crushed coriander seed
	5 large chillies (depending on their strength, and your preference)
	1 bunch fresh basil
	3 tbsp paprika
	2 bay leaves
	1 tbsp Cayenne pepper
	Greaseproof paper (if you are unsure of your jar lids)

If your courgettes are on the brink of marrowhood, scrape out the seeds as they might be a bit chewy.

Weigh the tomatoes, then skin them by making a cross shape with a knife on the bottom of each tomato and placing them in a bowl of boiling water. Leave for a minute then drain and the skins should peel off easily. Chop the tomatoes, leaving out any really tough core bits and place in the jam pan.

Weigh then de-seed and slice or chop the peppers (this depends what shape you want – I went for slivers of pepper and diced courgette), chop the courgette and aubergine and add to the jam pan.

Slice the onions and chillies finely, crush the garlic cloves with a little salt, crush the coriander seeds, measure the paprika and Cayenne pepper and add with the bay leaves to the jam pan.

Bring the veg mixture to the boil. Don't worry – although no liquid has been added the veg will give out their own. Reduce the heat to a simmer and cover with a lid to give the flavours time to start entwining. Stir occasionally until all the veg is soft, after about 45 minutes.

Bring back to the boil and boil hard for about 20 minutes uncovered to get rid of excess water.

Prepare your jars (cold oven 110°C / 225°F / Mk ¼ for 30 minutes) and tongs, lids, ladle, funnel and bubble-bursting knife (saucepan with boiling water for 20 seconds). Place the lids face down on a cake rack to dry and leave the funnel in the saucepan to keep warm. Cut out your greaseproof circles, if using them.

THE JAMMY BODGER

Don't pick too much fruit or too many different types of fruit as it can end up languishing in the bottom of your fridge.

Weigh your sugar, measure out the vinegar, and when the excess water has evaporated from the chutney, add them to the jam pan, stirring continuously until all the sugar has dissolved.

Increase the heat and stir occasionally to stop the chutney sticking. Take care as it boils like a volcano. Cook until there's no extra liquid on the surface and when you drag your spoon across the bottom of the jam pan it leaves a clear path. It should be only slightly more liquid than as you would eat it. Mine took about 45 minutes.

Ladle into the jars, dropping in whole basil leaves every now and then. Don't leave any on the top uncovered by chutney though.

Tap each jar on the work surface to encourage the chutney to settle and when all the jars are full, return to the first and examine it for air bubbles. If there are any, pierce them, then gently remove the knife.

Cover each pot with a circle of greaseproof paper (if using) and twist the lids on tightly.

Relax and eat in one month's time.

Taste Test: It's not vinegary at all and I love this mix of veg. It turns out so does everyone else, as within 1 month of it ripening (I'm not sure just what you call the chutney resting period), its all gone!

Mid-August: All the wild berry freebies including haws, hips, rowans, sloes and elderberries are out. Although the rowan berries are definitely getting sweeter, they are still inedible. Steve now tells me the raw rowan berry is in fact toxic, but fine once cooked. Like elderberries and haws they must only be mildly toxic. Sometimes the Internet is a bit melodramatic! It's another week yet for most berries, as they are only just changing colour, although there are some purply-black blackberries in more sheltered spots.

Apple or Plum Crumble Cake

I've made apple crumble cake twice in 2 weeks with Karma Colin's apples and each time it went down a storm.

Ingredients:	Crumble Topping:
300g / 2½ cups sliced eating or cooking apples OR 600g / 2½ cups pitted plums	½ tsp ground cinnamon
200g / 1 cup caster sugar (superfine)	130g / ⅝ cup brown sugar (the crunchy one)
200g / ⅞ cup (1¾ sticks) butter (at room temperature will make your life easier)	85g / ⅓ cup (¾ stick) butter (cold, if possible, then sliced into dice size pieces into the bowl)
200g / 1½ cups self raising flour	115g / 1 cup self raising or plain flour
4 eggs	1 handful chopped nuts (optional)
1½ tsp vanilla extract	

Preheat the oven to 180°C / 350°F / Mk 4 and grease a 21cm / 8½ inch round deep cake tin, or a similar sized square tin.

Keep your largest bowl for the creaming of the butter and make the crumble in whatever else you've got.

To make the crumble, add together the flour, brown sugar, cinnamon and butter in a bowl and rub through your fingers until it's like breadcrumbs (a few remaining bigger lumps are fine).

If using plums, rinse, slice in half and de-stone, and if using apples, peel, thinly slice and set them to one side.

Make the cake by creaming the butter and sugar until light and fluffy, then beat the eggs in, one at a time. Beat it loads if you want a lot of air in it and if it curdles, add a tbsp of the flour.

Stir in the vanilla, then sieve in ⅓ of the self raising flour and fold in gently (a figure of eight movement, repeated twice more until it's all gently folded in).

Arrange the apple slices or halved plums over the top and sprinkle over the crumble topping / nuts.

Bake in the oven for 45-50 minutes until an inserted skewer comes out clean and the topping is golden brown.

And so good warm with ice-cream!

Notes from a local jam maker

I have been making jams intermittently for quite a few years, primarily from wild blackberries, raspberries, elderberries, and sloes collected from hedgerows, but I also grow blackcurrants, redcurrants, gooseberries, and plums. Chutney making started when I grew too many vegetables. All this is quite a challenge as the Lake District has more than its fair share of rain.

My Mum taught me to make jam. She always bought lots of fruit from a farmer's stall when we went on day trips to Kent. I loved eating the jammy scum as soon as it was cool enough on bread and butter. I still do!

Friends and neighbours supply me with jars and lids in exchange for a full jar in return. My favourite jam is Victoria plum, closely followed by courgette and ginger. See what you think.

Courgette and Ginger Preserve

1kg / 8 cups chopped courgettes/zucchini

3 tbsp water

1110g / 5½ cups sugar

3 tbsp lemon juice

50g / 2oz root ginger, bruised (bash it with the side of a knife)

75g / 2½oz stem ginger finely chopped

Peel the courgettes and remove any seeds. Chop into 1cm cubes.

Put into the preserving pan with the water and cover and simmer for 20 minutes.

Put the bruised root ginger into a muslin bag and add to the cooked courgette together with the sugar, lemon juice and stem ginger.

Carry on as for normal jam making, but do remember to remove the muslin bag before potting.

Take the jam off the heat as soon as it is at setting point. If left on a hotplate it will continue cooking and become rather solid.

To test for set I put a few drops of boiling jam on a plate and leave them for exactly one minute. If a skin forms that wrinkles when pushed, the jam is ready.

This jam is very sticky and inclined to be the same consistency as golden syrup. It is delicious as the jam layer in a tray bake.

Tray Bake

Line a non-stick 28 x 18cm (11 x 7 inch) baking tray with shortcrust pastry. Spread jam thinly on the pastry. Whisk together 55g / ¼ cup (½ stick) butter, 55g / ¼ cup caster sugar, 55g / ½ cup self raising flour, 1 tsp milk, and 1 large egg for 1 minute and spread over the jam. Sprinkle with caster sugar and cook at 180°C / 350°F / Mk 4 for 30 minutes.

Any cake cooked in a baking tray can be called a tray bake, but the above recipe is what most people would expect. The sponge section can be any flavour, and the topping can be chopped nuts, spices, or fruit.

Mary Bass

SEPTEMBER

Notes from a local jam maker

My name is Elina and I'm married to Don, Mel's brother. We live in Lewes, East Sussex, right on the edge on the South Downs. We go for walks over the Downs, especially in the summer and autumn months, and pick a lot of blackberries and apples that grow in abundance. There are also a lot of mirabelle plums which are small, wild, yellow plums which are quite sour and make an excellent jam, especially if mixed with apples!

Whenever I think of pickling or making jam I ring my mother, Svetlana, first. She has been pickling and making jams for over 40 years. She lives in the Russian Caucasus where for many years fruit and veg were seasonal, so there was a lot of preserving and pickling activity come August and September. It's a little different now that more is available out of season. There is a lot of fruit here in England that grows in the Caucasus as well. My mother says that any fruit can be preserved if you add sugar to it, and almost any veg could be pickled just by adding salt and spices.

Sour Yellow Plum Jam

Prick the plums (but don't use sweet plums - it's just not the same), and boil in hot water for 2 minutes.

Drain the water, pour sugar syrup over them, and boil on a low heat for 20 minutes. Then let it cool down. (Incidentally, sugar syrups are covered in the Freezing section.)

Boil for another 20 minutes then let it cool down again.

Repeat once more, boiling it this time for 40 minutes, then put in jars.

To test for set I cool some down, stick my finger in the jam, and wobble it!

Sour Cherry Conserve

Take the pits out of the cherries and cover with sugar (1kg of fruit to 1kg of sugar).

Leave for about 5 hours.

Add 1 glass of water to each 1kg of fruit, and bring to the boil.

Boil for about an hour, taking off the foam as it forms.

Cool down, boil for another 1½ hours, then put in jars.

My worst mishap is jam spilling over the cooker. It's happened a few times, and its a bugger to clean after!

Also, like Mel I'm not a fan of pips and I usually pass any jam through a sieve to get rid of them, as they do tend to get stuck in your teeth!!

I've been for a walk with Svetlana over the Downs and she is amazing as she can identify every shrub and tree and tell you what to do with it for your health, for preserving and for generally good eating. Like Regula she has a wealth of knowledge of what is around us and how we can use it for our benefit, whilst still being kind to the plant.

Scratchy bushes, squishy berries, purple fingers = bramble jam. I've got 2 day old brambles (I think this is the name of the wild, not cultivated varieties) in the fridge, and Karma Colin's apples are fermenting nicely in the fruit bowl, so it's time to take action.

Bramble & Apple Jam

No. of jars: 7¾ large jars, yielding about 3.3kg	Ingredients
	1.1kg / 7½ cups blackberries
Time taken: 2 hours	700g / 6 cups apples, peeled and diced
	150ml / ⅔ cup or 350ml / 1½ cups water (use the larger amount for eating apples)
	2 tbsp lemon juice
	1.8kg / 9 cups granulated sugar

JAMMY TIP

Dice the apples smaller if using eating apples as they won't mulch like cooking apples and add a little more water if needed.

Brambles are too low in pectin for jamming, so are usually mixed with apples to give them a boost. You need to pre-soak the brambles in a bowl of water to kill off any critters before making jam. I thought you just rinsed the berries, but it's shocking the number of mini-bodies which rise out of the berries after soaking. The bramble, apple and elderberry mix makes an earthy flavoured autumnal jam (sorry, I just wanted to use the word) and adding lemon juice stops it looking muggy, helps the set and gives a flavourful tang.

Handy hint: If you are using small apples, weigh the apples after peeling and chopping as the weight will be considerably less than if weighed before.

How to Make

Commence drowning your blackberries in a bowl of water and soak for about 20 minutes. Peel and chop the apples and weigh and add them to the jam pan with the water.

Simmer the apples until soft, or completely pulpy if using cooking apples, usually about 20 minutes.

Prepare your jars (cold oven 110°C / 225°F / Mk ¼ for 30 minutes) and lids, ladle and funnel (saucepan with boiling water for 20 seconds). Place 3 saucers in the fridge to test for set

Drain and rinse the blackberries in a colander, then weigh and add to the jam pan.

When the blackberries are soft, after about 10 minutes, reduce the heat, add the lemon juice and the same weight of sugar as fruit, stirring well until all the sugar has completely dissolved.

Increase the heat and start testing for set.

When happy with the set, ladle into jars and twist on the lids.

Taste Test: I don't like the pippyness and picking bits out of my teeth. You can sieve the apples and

THE JAMMY BODGER

blackberries after they have softened, but then you have to treat it as a jelly and add 450g / 2¼ cups of sugar and 1 tbsp of lemon juice to each 600ml / 2½ cups of blackberry and apple juice. Maybe I just need to get over it. Blackberry jams use free fruit, set well and everyone seems to love them as they sell really well; obviously I have no taste.

Bramble Jam

Replace the apples with blackberries and have a little more lemon juice on standby in case the slightly heavy flavour needs a lift, or it struggles to set.

Bramble, Apple & Elderberry Jam

Use about **950g / 7½ cups apple, 350ml / 1½ cups water, 600g / 4¼ cups elderberries, 200g / 1⅓ cups blackberries, 1.75kg / 8¾ cups sugar** (the same weight as the total fruit), and **the juice of 2 small lemons**. Beware! This is a thick jam which erupts like a volcano, spitting at everything within arms' length.

Apple & Elderberry Jam

Add together 450g / 3½ cups peeled and diced apples, 145ml / ⅔ cup of water, 450g / 3¼ cups elderberries. Add the elderberries when the apples are completely mulched, then cook the elderberries for 10 minutes before adding 900g / 4½ cups sugar and 3 tbsp lemon juice.

A warming, fruity jam, and puréeing created a better texture. I still prefer blackberry, apple and elderberry jam though.

I had about 100g of elderberries left over and froze them in a little plastic pot to go with the frozen gooseberries at some point.

PS. The water variations in these recipes are down to whether I used cooking or eating apples, so just see how it goes. You don't want to have loads of water to boil off at the end, but at the same time your apples need enough to simmer down in - so strike the middle way and vary according to what your apples tell you.

Crab Apple Jelly

Just when I'd decided that crab apple trees were a thing of the past (not my past, but 'The Past'), Steve careers off the road in the car and stops by a gate, excitedly pointing to zillions of crab apples on a rather mature tree. We hastily collected the fruit as we were parked a bit precariously, and made a note to remember where we got them from for next year.

No. of jars : As I've reduced the recipe quantity I can't be 100% sure, but I think with a second straining you'd get 8 small jars, yielding about 1.9kg; not bad for jellies Time taken: Too long!	Ingredients 1.5kg / 13½ cups crab or cooking apples 1 litre / 4¼ cups water 1.5kg / 7½ cups granulated sugar (more than enough)
Calculating Sugar Formula: 600ml / 2½ cups juice = 450g / 2¼ cups sugar	

I tripled this recipe by simply simmering loads of apples and ladling more and more fruity pulp into the jelly bag. This was not a success as the sheer quantity of core and peel blocked the jelly bag so that the juice could not drain out. I also had to keep reheating the pulp left in the jam pan to keep it liquid enough to drip through, which meant that on a lovely sunny day I was stuck indoors. It then took overnight and half the following morning to drip through, and as the fruity pulp was still really moist I had to do a second straining.

I am NEVER using over 1.5kg / 3lb 5oz of apples again. The 'more fruit the merrier' method also failed as I didn't get as much jelly as I had hoped and had loads of apple pulp from the jelly bag left that was blatantly still juicy. I'm ashamed to say that after two days of languishing in the fridge most of it met its maker on the compost heap, although I did reheat one batch with more water, pushed it through a seive and made apple spiced tea cake – see the next recipe.

Be careful the ladle doesn't dribble directly into the juice bowl. If this happens take take a deep breath and empty the juice bowl back into the jam pan and start ladling through again; no-one wants a cloudy jelly.

How to Make

Stage 1

Rinse the apples and pull out the stalks. Roughly chop them and put them in the jam pan complete with pips, cores, and peel. Cover with the water.

Simmer gently until the apples are completely soft, squidging them with the back of the wooden spoon to make sure.

Scald the jelly bag, then set up the stand and bowl.

When the apples are mulchy, ladle them into the jelly bag and leave until the juice stops dripping or overnight.

Stage 2 – second straining

Empty the jelly bag back into the CLEAN jam pan, add 500ml / 2⅛ cups of water and simmer again until completely mulchy.

Rinse the jelly bag out, scald it again, then hang it from the jelly bag stand.

Ladle the fruity pulp into the jelly bag and leave it to drip through until it stops dripping.

Stage 3

Prepare your jars and place 3 saucers in the fridge to test for set (I'm sure you know the rules by now!).

Remove the jelly bag and stand and empty the jelly bag into the composter or bin.

Measure the juice and use the Calculating Sugar Formula to calculate the amount of sugar needed.

Pour the juice into the jam pan and, when warm, add the sugar, stirring continuously until it has all dissolved.

Increase the heat and when the jelly is boiling rapidly all over the surface and making a popping sound, start testing for set. Remove the jam pan from the heat each time you test.

When you are happy with the set, ladle the jelly into the jars and twist the lids on tightly.

Leave the jars on a cake rack to cool.

Taste Test: Really good and much better than I'd anticipated. Regula is going to use it to baste a posh apple tart whilst the rest of us are enjoying its tangyness on toast.

Apple Spiced Tea Cake

Ingredients

60ml / ¼ cup (½ stick) melted butter

1 egg

250ml / 1 cup apple sauce

125g / ⅔ cup mix of granulated / dark brown (Muscovado) / soft light brown sugar

225g / 1¾ cups plain flour

2 tsp baking powder

½ tsp bicarbonate of soda

½ tsp salt

2 tsp allspice

100g / ⅔ cup (packed) raisins

175g / 1 cup chopped nuts

How to Make

Grease a standard loaf tin. Melt the butter in a small saucepan. Beat the eggs lightly in a large mixing bowl, then add the apple sauce, melted butter and sugar. Mix everything together.

Preheat the oven to 180°C / 350°F / Mk 4.

Sieve in the bicarbonate of soda, baking powder, salt and spices, then sieve in the flour a bit at a time so that you mix it in a couple of times before the sieve is empty. Stir in the raisins and nuts.

Pour (actually more of a plop) into the tin and bake for about 1 hour or until an inserted skewer comes out clean, with no sticky cake on it.

Remove the cake from the oven and let it shrink back from the tin before serving. This makes it easier to get out of the tin. Really great warm, but I think I say that about all cakes.

Wild Plum Jam

Plum, plum, plum, plum and even more plum...

Plum recipes say that the stones rise to the surface and then you simply skim them off. But what if they don't? Nobody wants stones in their jam. I de-stoned each plum, which sounds like a chore but was actually quite fun, a little like podding broad beans. If you know the type of plums you've got then name the jam after them ie. Victoria plum jam.

I've since realised that other plums stones do NOT squidge out easily. In fact some refuse to give them up at all, so see the following plum recipes.

Beware cuppers! Some of the plum quantities are in pounds and ounces as it's too tricky to work out the cuppage volume for whole plums with their stones in.

No. of jars: 8 medium jars, yielding approximately 2.6kg Time taken: 2 hours (not including picking), as it took a long time to reach setting point	**Ingredients** 2kg / 4lb 7oz plums 855ml / 3½ cups water 2 large lemons (juice only – about 6 tbsp) 2kg / 10 cups granulated sugar

How to Make

First prep the plums. Weigh then rinse them in a colander. Have a large bowl for the plums and another small bowl for the stones and play squidging the stones out. This might be easier with the cherry

THE JAMMY BODGER

stoner, but I was quite happy firing them around the kitchen.

Place the plums and water in the jam pan, bring to the boil, then simmer until the plums are soft. Keep an eye out for any stones you've missed rising to the surface.

Prepare your jars (cold oven 110°C / 225°F / Mk ¼ for 30 minutes) and lids, ladle and funnel (saucepan with boiling water for 20 seconds). Place 3 saucers in the fridge to test for set.

When the plums are soft, weigh and add the sugar, stirring continuously until dissolved.

When dissolved, add the lemon juice.

Increase the heat, and when you've tested for set, remove the jam and pot.

Taste Test: A delicate but fabulously fruity flavour, not bold and brash, but definitely one of my favourites. I might have decided before I tasted it that it was going to be a favourite, as free fruit makes a cheap jam.

Plums again and I can't believe it. What you read in the jammy books actually happens. Through the local grapevine people are contacting me to let me know they have plums or apples available that I can have if I pick them and give them a couple of jars of jam in return. I didn't think this actually happened in real life, so I'm excited at the prospect of free fruit, but the pressure of making jam for people who've possibly made it for years is a bit daunting.

Plum & Vanilla Jam

As for the previous recipe but with **1.37kg / 8¼ cups plums** (stones taken out), an equal quantity of sugar, the **juice of 1 lemon** and **1 tbsp vanilla** added.

Damson Jam

Plums are not created equal. There are different types of plum; cooking and dessert, and damsons are cooking plums and have a higher level of pectin.

No. of jars: 4 *medium jars, yielding about 1.3kg*	Ingredients
	650g / 1½ lb damsons, approx 700ml / 3 cups water
	About 550g / 3¼ cups sugar

Nearly cover the damsons with water, then soften them for about 30 minutes, mashing them completely with a potato masher. Scoop out the damson stones and keep them in a small bowl. Put the stones in a seive and hold them over the jam pan. Pour a small amount of boiling water over them, then rub them to get the rest of the plummy juice off, and don't forget to scrape off the back of the seive. Then weigh the stones and deduct the weight of the stones from the weight of the damsons, and add this amount of sugar. Any missed stones should float to the surface after the sugar is added, so keep your eyes open and stir to encourage them to the surface.

The jam set very well with no scum. As it's very thick be careful it doesn't burn on the bottom of the jam pan, and if using a small quantity such as this, use a standard jam pan, stock pot, or cauldron.

Taste Test: Damson Jam is punchy, more like a blackcurrant jam, and all the plum jams have a flavour unique to the individal plum used.

Lessons Learnt while Plumming

I don't want to see another plum / greengage or whatever you want to call them until... err next year.

The plums go a horrible brown if you pull the stalks out but don't make jam straight away, so don't do it!

Plums are best kept on the tree until the last minute as they don't keep well. They are even worse than strawberries.

Just eat or freeze over-ripe fruit. Don't make jam unless you use jam sugar as it will be really difficult to set.

If you want to use a plum recipe that says 'stones out,' but your stones are tough to remove, increase the amount of plums by about 200g/2¼ cups per 900g/5½ cups to allow for the loss of stone weight.

There is nothing wrong with a loose set ('slippery') plum jam. Just say it's the type of plums.

Flavourings to Add whilst Simmering

A couple of cinnamon sticks, but remove them before potting, or plum kernels to boost the flavour. I tried to crack the stones to remove the kernels, but kept bashing the kernels to smithereens. We counted them in and out of the jam to make sure we got them all out, but I'm not sure they added anything to the flavour. The kernels taste of chewy marzipan!

How much fruit is too much fruit? I've now got even more plums as my neighbours can't cope with their glut, and suddenly neither can I. I've given some away and started looking into different methods of freezing.

I froze 700g / 4 cups of plums, the amount needed for plum crumble cake. I cut the plums in half, de-stoned them, squirted them with a bit of lemon juice, stirred them over, bagged them, then wrote on the bag the type of fruit and the weight. I then froze 900g/5½ cups in the same way, as I think this is about the right weight for a fruit pie.

THE JAMMY BODGER

I also froze plums in syrup. I made a sugar syrup by dissolving 200g / 1cup of sugar in 600ml / 2½ cups of water for every 450g / 2¾ cups of plums, so quite a heavy one.

I sliced and froze apples on trays, then scraped them off the trays into plastic bags. Be careful what trays you use. I used clean oven trays, but some of the black came off the trays onto the apples. I now have clean oven trays, so that's a bonus. Now I prefer to just use a plastic serving tray to freeze fruit on before bagging it. Freezing this way keeps the fruit separate, so that you can take it out as you need it.

Boozy Plums

No. of jars: 4 medium jars, but one only half full of fruit. I needed to portion the fruit out more equally. Yield about 1kg Time taken: About 2 hours	Ingredients
	900g / 2lb just ripe plums (any type, about 14)
	600ml / 2½ cups brandy
	The rind of 1 orange, peeled in a long strip (or 2 if it breaks off)
	350g / 1¾ cups granulated or caster sugar (superfine)
	4 or 5 star anise

With the deluge of plums that don't seem too keen to part with their stones, a recipe where you don't have to remove them suddenly seems a very good idea. With most bottled fruits you need to sterilise the jars again after potting, which sounds like a lot of faff, but if your fruit is bottled in pure alcohol, at least 40% proof, a second sterilising is not required. All reasonably priced brandy (ie. cheap) is 36% proof, and the price difference for over 40% is massive – we`re talking from £6.50 for 35cl to £25. Common sense and tight purse strings prevail on this one.

Bottled fruits can be stored for up to 6 months or 1 year, depending on who you believe. I ate mine at Christmas and they were fab. There are two main methods: poach the fruit in a sugar / booze syrup, remove the fruit, reduce the syrup, pour it over again and pot. Or alternatively, prick and pack the fruit into sterilised jars, pour over the sugar and brandy, then give the pot a quick shake every time you pass it. (Think of Barry Manilow shaking his maracas!)

Make sure the plums are fully submerged with more syrup on top. If the plums rise to the top, give the jar a twizzle each time you walk past to try and sink them under.

How to Make

Pick the stalks off and weigh your plums – no bruises or blemishes please – then rinse and drain in a colander

Pierce the plums with a fork. This will hopefully stop the skins bursting.

Prep your jars (cold oven 110°C / 225°F / Mk ¼ for 30 minutes) and lids, ladle and funnel (saucepan with boiling water for 20 seconds).

Measure the brandy and sugar, pour into the jam pan with the orange rind and star anise and heat gently, stirring until the sugar has dissolved.

Tip the plums gently into the jam pan and poach for about 10 minutes, or until soft. Take one out and squish it to make sure.

With a slotted spoon, remove the plums and divide equally between the jars. They need to be full to the jars' shoulders. If there is juice in the jars, tip it back into the jam pan.

Pop the filled jars back into the oven to keep warm.

Boil the syrup hard until it has reduced by a third. Beware! The line around the jam pan is the level of the liquid when the plums were in, so it's a third down from the level **after** the plums have been removed, **not** the top line. Then strain through a nylon sieve into a jug and pour over the plums. The syrup should cover the plums and not leave any space for air. You might need to jiggle the plums about a bit or prod them with the tongs, to make them settle.

Screw the lids on tightly and leave to cool.

Label and store for 2 months before eating, and eat within a year.

Taste Test: I'm going to have to come back and fill this in after a couple of months, although I can already vouch for the flavour of the brandy syrup, and it didn't need an ice cream accompaniment.

Taste Test 2: Over Christmas I ate the plums with ice cream and placed the leftover syrup in the fridge. Plum heaven! Those were Steve's words as we drank the syrup on New Year's Eve, although he doesn't realise the alcohol content and is getting a bit talkative. Damsons in brandy were the definitely the best.

Greengage Conserve

So what's the difference between a plum and a greengage? Greengages seem to be a posh type of plum, much heralded for their flavour. They look like a yellow or green plum, and pardon my French but they have a pronounced crack in their bottom.

A nearby greengage tree's fruit is now ripe, so I grab 3 punnets and head off. But I've been beaten to it by someone or something (possibly deer related), as all the lower accessible branches are empty and I'm reduced to jumping up and down in a most ungainly fashion and grabbing at random branches.

I only get about 10 and when I try one it looks and tastes the same as all the plums I've been given. As I chew and mull this over, a maggot crawls out the other half of the plum / greengage and into my hand. Suddenly the plums at home seem much more enticing and I'm now (conveniently) completely convinced some are greengages. I'm going to attempt a conserve if they de-stone easy.

De-stoning took an hour as I had to delicately slice the greengages in half and give them a gentle twist to release the stone whilst trying to keep them in good shape. You need to squirt lemon juice over the greengages before the sugar has been added, otherwise the cut side goes a manky brown.

Handy hint: Try to simmer the greengages slowly and not for too long to help retain their shape and texture.

You are looking for the conserve to set loosely, not as firmly as jam, so it doesn't need such a manic boil; think rapid but controlled.

	Ingredients
No. of jars: 4 tall jars plus a half jar taster, yielding approximately 1.4kg	1kg / 6 cups greengages or plums (weight after stoning)
Time taken: 1 hour at the start, then 1 hour bringing to the boil and setting	1kg / 5 cups granulated sugar
	1 lemon, juiced

How to Make

Stage 1

Rinse the greengages, slice them in half top to tail and place in a large bowl sitting on the weighing scales.

When you have 1kg of fruit, stir in 1 tsp of lemon juice and weigh, then stir in the sugar.

Make sure the greengages are completely coated in the sugar, then cover and leave to marinate for 2-3 hours.

Stage 2

Prepare your jars (cold oven 110°C / 225°F / Mk ¼ for 30 minutes) and lids, ladle and funnel (saucepan with boiling water for 20 seconds). Place 3 saucers in the fridge to test for set.

Pour the fruit and sugar gloop into the jam pan and warm gently until the sugar has dissolved, stirring continuously.

Increase the heat and add the rest of the lemon juice and (if you want to) the kernels of some of the greengages. If using kernels, count how many you put in. Don't stir, and aim for a rapid, steady boil. We are looking to set, but it will be a loose set.

Test your conserve for set using the saucers and it needs to just stay apart.

When you are happy with the set, take the jam pan off the heat and wait a couple of minutes for the fruit to settle. Then remove the kernels, if added, and start skimming off the scum. It's a bit difficult as whole bits of fruit will be floating to the surface, but get most of the scum off, then stir gently in one direction to disperse the rest.

Leave to stand for 15 minutes, letting the conserve

thicken slightly, then stir to disperse the fruit, ladle into jars and twist the lids on tightly. Place on a cake rack to cool.

When cool, wipe down, label the jars and store in a cool, dark place.

Taste Test: This is the best of all the plum jams, probably because it's not a jam but a conserve! I think it's also the greengage flavour as well, which bursts into your mouth.

Apple Juicing

Wow! I am impressed at how very organised we are. (That's the royal we, by the way. I was messing around in the kitchen at the time.) Regula, Steve and friends used an apple press at Mill House Cider Museum in Owermoigne, a nearby village, to make loads of apple juice. It only costs £15 an hour to use the press and you can pay £30 each for these massive 50 litre plastic containers to keep the juice in. As the apple press presses the whole apple, including the core, pips and all, the fibre level is high and it tastes great. You take the apple juice home and decant it into bottles. The bottles can be clean milk cartons or any bottles with lids.

Defrosting Strawberry Freezer Jam

I fancy something other than plums, so I defrost the freezer jam I made in July. It's not like jam at all. It hasn't got the jellified texture as it's just a fresh fruit purée. It tastes great, but it's not jam. Other freezer jam recipes use jam sugar and I'll perhaps try one of those next year.

Sweet n' Hot Pepper Jam

I fancy making a kind of antipasti jar of roast sweet peppers, so I bought 18 peppers for £5 at the market. I wanted big fat strips of peppers like you often get with fajitas, and used ½ jam sugar and ½ granulated, as that's what I had in my cupboard, and bought a jar of reduced price Jalapeño chillies; ah, the last of the big spenders.

No. of jars: 5 medium jars, yielding about 1.6 kg *Time taken: 2 hours, but I did simmer the peppers for too long*	**Ingredients**
	1.5kg / 14 cups sliced peppers, a rainbow of colours if possible
	200g / 1 cup chopped chillies OR a whole jar of Jalapeño chillies and their vinegar too
	1 tbsp paprika
	1 crushed garlic clove
	550ml / 2⅓ cups white wine
	1.5kg / 7½ cups jam sugar (or granulated sugar and 1 pectin sachet, or ½ bottle of liquid pectin, with no need for extra lemon)
	75ml / ⅓ cup lemon Juice
	1½ tsp salt
	A twist of pepper

How to Make

Rinse then cut the peppers in half, removing the seeds and slicing them to the size you want. Slice the chillies finely, crush the garlic and measure the paprika and the vinegar. Put everything into the jam pan and heat gently until you get a rolling boil.

THE JAMMY BODGER

Don't simmer the peppers for too long, otherwise they end up overcooked and look like crinkly worms floating in syrup. Do boil them HARD though after the sugar has dissolved.

Prepare your jars (cold oven 110°C / 225°F / Mk ¼ for 30 minutes) and lids, ladle and funnel (saucepan with boiling water for 20 seconds).

Weigh and add the sugar (and pectin sachets if using), stirring continuously until the sugar has dissolved. Add the lemon juice and the salt and pepper.

Boil the peppers hard for 5 minutes, then remove from the heat. (This is the time to add liquid pectin).

Allow to cool slightly for 5-10 minutes so the mixture jellifies a little, and you can stir to distribute the peppers evenly.

Ladle into the jars and seal.

When cool, label and store in a dark place. This will keep for up to 8 months.

Taste Test: Later in the year at the chutney tasting this was even voted better than Mediterranean chutney by some pepper lovers. We've eaten this with roasted veg, as a side dollop to go with mackerel and in a wrap. Basically we ate it with anything until it ran out. I wish I had a photo of it, but we really ate it too quickly. It's that good!

Taste of Autumn Chutney

The fruit and veg used can be any mix of whatever you've got to hand which is fresh and fruity, and the more variety the better. Just keep the total weight the same. The preparation takes forever and I keep having to remind myself to cut small.

No. of jars: 15 small jars, about 3.6kg	Ingredients
Time taken: All day at home, but not all day working; long periods were spent sitting and reading a book *Unfortunately some recipes are based on the pre-chopped weight of a mix of fruit and veg, making an American cup comparison extremely tricky, and at best a guess, or at worst a lie. I have therefore included an Imperial weight measurement instead, so cast aside your cups and embrace the scales!!!*	2kg / 4 lb 6oz mixed fruit and veg (apple, marrow/courgette, cauliflower florets, carrot, swede, pear, plum, and a few blackberries) 675g / 3¾ cups chopped onions 450g / 2½ cups green or red tomatoes. Don't worry about skinning any green toms 750ml / 3¼ cups red wine vinegar 2 tsp each of chillies, coriander seeds, peppercorns, mustard seeds, dried chillies, and any warming spices you fancy 2 crushed garlic cloves 450g / 2cups sugar (dark or light brown) 450g / 3 cups raisins or dates

How to Make

Step 1 flavouring the vinegar

Slice your onions, measure the vinegar and prep your spices. Some, like the coriander seeds, are best given a bash in the pestle and mortar to help release their flavour, but you don't need to pulp them as they are going in the spice bag.

Tie up your spices in a spice bag, tying the string tightly, and if there's lots of muslin left over, trim it and any straggling string.

Pour half the vinegar into the jam pan and add the onions, garlic, any spices which are going directly into the pan and the spice bag, and simmer for 15 minutes, then remove from the heat, cover and leave. You are encouraging the spices to infuse.

Step 2 the remaining prep

Put the radio on! You are going to be chopping for some time. Peel and core the apples and pears, stone any plums, peel the marrow and remove the seeds, but any courgettes can keep both. Try to chop everything about the same size. I prep one type, weigh it, note the weight, add it to the jam pan, then start on the next one.

Add all the fruit and veg and the remaining vinegar and simmer until soft for at least 45 minutes.

Turn down the heat, add the sugar and stir until dissolved.

Add the raisins or dates, then clean up!!

Prepare your jars (cold oven 110°C / 225°F / Mk ¼ for 30 minutes) and lids, ladle, funnel and bubble bursting knife (saucepan with boiling water for 20 seconds). If you are using greaseproof paper, draw and cut out your circles.

Step 3 turning the vinegar and veg into chutney

Increase the heat and stir frequently so the bottom of the pan doesn't burn. Continue until you can draw a wooden spoon over the surface and it leaves a gash for a couple of seconds / or you scrape a spoon along the bottom and it leaves a clear trail / or just cook until it is thick and glossy with no visible liquid, or nearly as thick as you would like to eat it.

Step 4 potting

Remove the spice bag and bin it, or leave to cool, untie, bin the spices, and wash the muslin in washing up liquid to use again.

Ladle the chutney into the jars and after filling each jar, tap it firmly on the work surface to try to encourage it to settle, then remove any bubbles with the bubble bursting knife and top up any jars which fall short.

Twist the lids on tightly, wipe down the jars and place on a cake rack.

When cold, label and store in a dark place for at least a month before tasting.

Taste test: It's weird because when you taste a chutney immediately after cooking it tastes really vinegary, and that's about it. You can't actually taste any spices as the flavour hasn't developed, so what should it taste like now, and is it right??

Taste Test 2: A couple of months later this chutney looks great and tastes good; not hot, but just a mild chutney which most people like. I think it needs more heat, and not just a chilli heat, but a warmth, perhaps more cumin and coriander, and yes why not more chilli too, so feel free to add more.

Now is a good time to freeze some blackberries or apples for later in the year when you aren't so busy. You could freeze 1 or 2kg of blackberries for making drunken berry jelly (see the January recipe) or 500g for making a curd. Frozen apples are always handy for making jellies, jams, a people pleasing apple crumble or...

Eve's Pudding

Ingredients

500g / 4 cups apples (sliced), or any other fruit

1 tbsp Demerara sugar

75g / ⅓ cup caster or granulated sugar

150g / 1¼ cups self raising flour

75g / ⅓ cup (⅔ stick) butter

1 egg

Grated rind of lemon (optional)

A splash of milk

How to Make

Slice the fruit into a greased ovenproof dish and add the lemon rind, if using, and a little extra sugar if the fruit needs sweetening.

Cream the butter and caster / granulated sugar, adding the egg a little at a time and folding in the flour. Add enough milk until it drops off the spoon and looks like cake mixture.

Sprinkle with Demerara sugar.

Bake in the oven at 180ºC / 350ºF / Mk 4 for 40-45 minutes.

You can add ground almonds to the flour or sprinkle them on top. I think this is the same as upside down cake.

Mid-September: I haven't thought about vegetables for jam, but you get carrot cake, chocolate and beetroot cake, pumpkin pie and pumpkin cake, so really some vegetables are just as sweet as fruit. As Regula Guru's got about 70 marrows, which are at their best now, with no need for any of that pre-salting lark, it's time to make the most of the glut and make some jam.

Marrow & Ginger Jam

It's taken me a while to build up to this, as frankly I'm not sure if I'm going to like it. As I was faffing around in the kitchen distractedly I gave this ages to simmer down, stirring and mashing it every now and then to prevent it sticking. Suddenly it was 9.00pm and I wanted to make dinner, so naughtily I shoved a couple of pectin sachets in to make it set quicker as I couldn't believe that marrow could set well as it doesn't contain pectin. If you add the juice of 4 lemons the jam will only need a little added pectin.

Handy hint: If you are struggling for set you can add pectin sachets or some liquid pectin, but ideally wait until you are actually struggling, not just because you want some dinner.

Amend this recipe according to how much marrow you've got. I had a lot and also have a large jam pan. You can make this   in a small pan with as little as 450g of marrow,   1 or 2 cooking apples

THE JAMMY BODGER

and the juice of just 1 lemon.

Stir frequently until the marrow has given out some of its juices.

You need some muslin and string to tie up the root ginger, or add 1½ tbsp of chopped crystallized or preserved ginger.

No. of jars: 12½ medium jars, yielding about 4kg Time taken: About 5 hours, but could have been done in 3	Ingredients
	2kg / 15 cups cubed marrow (winter squash)
	600g / 5 cups cooking apples (needs to be cookers for the higher pectin level)
	70g / 2½oz / ¾ cup root ginger, bashed or finely sliced (or chopped crystallized or preserved ginger)
	2.6kg / 13 cups granulated sugar
	The juice of 4 lemons
	300ml / 1¼ cups pectin stock OR 1 sachet of bought pectin added with the sugar

How to Make

Chop the ends off the marrow, cut it in half lengthways (if large), then sit it upright on the chopping board and peel with a sharp knife. De-seed with a spoon and chop into cubes.

Peel the apples and chop into cubes.

Simmer the apples and marrow, (and finely chopped crystallised ginger if using) gently in the jam pan, stirring occasionally if sticking, until soft.

Prep your jars (cold oven 110°C / 225°F / Mk ¼ for 30 minutes) and lids, ladle and funnel (saucepan with boiling water for 20 seconds). Place 3 saucers in the fridge to test for set.

Mash the apple and marrow with a potato masher until almost puréed when really soft and add the lemon juice.

Peel the root ginger and then bash with the side of the knife to bruise it. Slice it if you wish. Wrap it in muslin, knot tightly with string and place in the pan.

Increase the heat until simmering, then remove from the heat and stir in the sugar (and pectin sachets, if using).

Boil hard for about 20 minutes. If using liquid pectin remove from the heat after 5 minutes of hard boiling, add the pectin and stir in. It should be ready to pot, but if not, heat again. Stand well back when stirring as it's positively volcanic when thick. (Stir in home-made pectin stock at this point, if using.)

Look to set the jam, although with thick jams it can be quite difficult to tell. When it sits like jam on the saucer, it's set.

Taste Test: I didn't expect to, but I really like this. I didn't think it would actually taste like a jam, but it certainly does. It's neither sickly sweet nor in your face and has a lovely balanced flavour. It sounds as if I'm now patronising my own jam, but it really is 'nice.'

JAMMY TIP

Keep any empty vinegar bottles if they clean up okay as they can be used for sloe gin or cordial next year. Any bottles will do as long as the cap is OK and the mouth of the bottle is wide enough to pop a sloe in.

Late September: Once again a walk on a sunny day with Regula and her dog Jim at our heels (until you lose him for 20 minutes when he's off chasing rabbit odours) is enough to re-enthuse any jam maker. The hedges and bushes are bowing under the weight of unpicked fruit, begging to be unburdened and I know just the jelly for the job. I've got a plastic bag in my pocket and I'm not afraid to use it. In go sloes, a few blackberries, rosehips and haws. Although I think haws are bland there are loads of them and maybe the flavour will blossom and balance the tartness of the sloes.

Hedgerow Fruits Jam

No. of jars: 8 medium jars, yielding about 2.6kg	Ingredients
	1.5kg / 3lb 5oz sloes, haws, blackberries, rosehips, and elderberries
Time taken: 4 hours approximately	1.5 litre / 6⅓ cups water – or enough to cover
I have a large jam pan – no I'm not boasting, just saying you may need to halve this recipe	1.5kg / 3lb 5oz / 12 cups chopped apples (eating or cooking apples)
	2 kg / 10 cups granulated sugar
	2 lemons (about 6 tbsp lemon juice)
Calculating Sugar Formula: 600ml / 2½ cups juice = 450g / 2¼ cups sugar + 2 tbsp lemon juice	

If you call it a jelly people ask what to do with it, so I'm thinking about calling all jellies that taste great on toast jams, after all a no-bits-of-shred marmalade is still called a marmalade (I'm not sure if I follow my own reasoning here).

The first batch of jelly / jam was bland, so I tried again

THE JAMMY BODGER

with more blackberries and sloes. Some of the sloes have a bluish blush, but this is perfectly normal and just rinses off.

How to Make

Stage 1

Pick your fruit then rinse and pick-over all your berries. If they are all mixed in, soak the lot in bowls of water for 10 minutes and drain off any funny stuff that floats to the surface. If the blackberries have been picked separately just soak them and rinse the rest.

Rinse then drain and weigh the fruit and place in the jam pan.

Prep your apples. If they need peeling, peel and place in a bowl of water with lemon juice. If they don't, rinse well to remove any dirty bits and the stalk, but keep the core and pips for the added pectin.

Dice the apples, core, pips and all, weigh (roughly the same weight of apples and berries), then place in the jam pan with the water and bring to a gentle boil.

Reduce the heat and simmer the fruit for about 1 hour until pulpy. Help it along by giving it a good mash.

Scald your jelly bag and set up the stand. Ladle the fruity pulp into the jelly bag, watching for any cheeky drips from the ladle.

Leave the jelly bag to drip through, ideally overnight, but if not then for at least a couple of hours, or until it stops dripping.

Stage 2

Prep your jars (cold oven 110°C / 225°F / Mk ¼ for 30 minutes) and lids, ladle and funnel (saucepan with boiling water for 20 seconds). Place 3 saucers in the fridge to test for set.

Pour or ladle the juice from the bowl into a measuring jug, note the amount of juice and using the Calculating Sugar Formula beneath the Ingredients, work out how much sugar to add.

Warm the juice in the jam pan and when just simmering add the sugar, stirring continuously until dissolved.

Add the lemon juice (2 tbsp for every 600ml / 2½ cups of juice, or just 1 tbsp if you have used cooking or crab apples).

Increase the heat and look to set the jelly.

When the jelly is boiling continuously (but not rising up the pan) and making a popping sound, hold the wooden spoon on one side and see if it drips in clotted, jellified lumps. If it does then move the pan off the heat and test for set on the saucer.

When you are happy with the set, take the pan off the heat and wait a minute for the jelly to settle, then skim off the scum for all you are worth. It's easier when the jelly is slightly set (but if the jelly sets hard in the jam pan you can warm it gently again before potting).

Ladle into the jars, screw the lids on tightly, wipe down the jars and place on a cake rack.

Taste Test: Tart and sweet – just how a jelly / jam should be. The sloes and lemon juice do their work, with the others as back up flavours.

OCTOBER

650ml / 2¾ cups cider vinegar (although I have used other vinegars)

500g / 3⅛ cups chopped onions

500g / 3 cups (packed) sultanas

3 tsp salt

4 or 5 cloves (I use whole ones)

1 tsp allspice

1 tsp black peppercorns (I have used ground)

I live with my wife Linda and two children, or teenagers should I say, Lauren and James in Buckinghamshire. I am the garden man in my household. We are lucky we have a fair sized garden in which I have a vegetable plot and a number of fruit trees. I am also blessed with 2 sheds. One has a fridge, heating, and a woodworking bench with tools etc. and chairs too. The other is more for storage and has all the gardening gear in it; lawnmower, power washer etc.

I always have too many apples to either eat or store, and this is a good way of using the surplus.

It's best made as soon as the apples and plums are available, which may mean storing the plums carefully for a short while; pick them early, keep them cool, and separated, or you can buy a few and cheat.

Plum & Apple Chutney

1kg / 2lb 4oz plums

1kg / 2lb 4oz apples

500g / 2¼ cups (packed) soft Demerera sugar

Warm the sugar for 30 minutes in a low oven.

Core, chop and peel the apples.

Remove the stones and halve the plums.

Place the fruit, vinegar, onions, sultanas, and spices in a large saucepan, bringing them to a boil and then simmering for 30 minutes.

Stir in the warm sugar until smooth, then boil. Immediately turn it down to a simmer, and stir every 5 to 10 minutes to ensure there is no sticking to the pan.

When it has thickened, cool and then put into jars.

It should be sealed and left for 8 to 10 weeks before use, but will keep for a long time.

Richard du Plessis

My flat smells of fermenting fruit (yes, still!) and not in a pleasant way. So I make up some apple sauce for the freezer.

Apple Sauce

500g / 1lb 2oz apples (about 3⅔ cups)

2-3 tbsp water

25g / ⅛ cup (¼ stick) butter

A sprinkle of sugar

How to Make

Peel and slice the apples and cook with the water until completely pulpy, then beat with a wooden spoon until smooth-ish and beat in the butter.

Add a little sprinkle of sugar.

When cool this can be frozen and then defrosted to make apple spiced tea cake (see the recipe in September after crab apple jelly). Serve with roast meat or sweeten it and fill a tart case, then cover it with custard and bake. Alternatively you could make a crumble or Eve's pudding, or for a quick pudding stir it into custard, place in the fridge for 30 minutes and claim it's a fruit fool!

The pumpkins in the field have been quietly growing humongous. We haven't been over to 'the far side' (sounds like over to the 'Dark Side') of the field much, as the summer glut of produce is all in the closer plots. But unbeknown to me a multitude of different pumpkins of every size, shape and colour have been slowly growing larger day by day, all nestling amongst a web of triffid-like tubing which stretches and intertwines over the whole massive plot.

The Pumpkin Festival is held every year at The Square and Compass pub, and attracts loads of tourists, walkers and locals. We turn up on the day to see the massive pumpkins being taken from the backs of Land Rovers; some are covered in blankets either to keep them warm or to protect them from prying eyes.

I'm selling my jams and chutneys and they sell much better than I'd expected, although I'm always surprised at people's choices; I thought bramble jelly would sell better than bramble jam, but few people share my aversion to pips. People definitely prefer more traditional chutneys with lots of different fruit.

I also seem to be attracting other jam ladies who study my jars for ages and then admit they are looking for recipe ideas and checking out my labels (well done Labels Liz). I'm happy to chat and swap recipe ideas, but whenever I mention a jam swap they seem to baulk at the suggestion. I think jam ladies have a certain pride in their produce, so to offer to swap might mean they are missing a flavour -either that or they just think mine look rubbish.

I'm also more honest about mine. Some are labelled very truthfully like 'Slippery Plum.' Well why not? It tastes great, but the plums were over-ripe. I don't think I've got anything to be embarrassed about. You don't need to be making it for 20 years to be able to make a jar of jam.

By early afternoon I can't feel my fingers. I've borrowed a pair of fingerless gloves, but it's no good. My selling spirit is broken, so I pack up and head off leaving Regula to stick it out for another couple of hours. This is definitely a do again event, although it seems strange not to have any jam. I'm now a jam lady with no jam.

Tongue Tingling Tomato Chutney and Cheeky Chappy's Tomato Chutney

I made two different versions, one chutney trying to be hot! hot! hot! and one more warm and traditional. I meant to add 200g of dates, but when I opened the pack I realised they were sugar coated and crunchy, so I thought they might go slimy in the pan.

If you want to add dates or raisins, simply add about 200g / 1¼ cups (packed) and reduce the quantity of tomatoes by the same amount.

No. of jars: 12 small jars, yielding approximately 2.9kg	Ingredients
	2.75kg / 15 cups green or red tomatoes
	500g / 3⅛ cups red or brown onions, or a mixture (weight after chopping)
Time taken: about 4 hours, but for a lot of that time the chutney was simmering away	20 chillies (or 5 if you prefer it mild)
	15 cardamom pods (or 8 plus a tbsp crushed coriander seeds)
	2 tbsp mild chilli spice or paste (or leave this out)
	6 garlic cloves, crushed (or less if you don't like garlic)
	570ml / 2½ cups apple cyder vinegar
	450g / 2 cups (packed) Demerara sugar (or any sugar)
	Salt and pepper

How to Make

Chop the onions, then weigh and place in the jam pan with the rinsed, weighed and chopped tomatoes. Add 1 tbsp of salt, mix in, cover and leave to stand for an hour (unheated as this draws out their water and then they can cook in it).

Crush the garlic with a little salt, slice the chillies, remove the cardamom seeds from the pods and bash to a fine powder in the pestle and mortar.

Weigh the sugar and measure out the vinegar.

When the tomatoes and onions have soaked, add all the spices, garlic and vinegar. Simmer until the tomatoes and onions are soft.

Reduce the heat, add the sugar and stir continuously until completely dissolved

Prep your jars (cold oven 110°C /225°F / Mk ¼ for 30 minutes) and lids, ladle, funnel and bubble bursting knife (saucepan with boiling water for 20 seconds). Cut out your greaseproof circles too, if using.

Increase the heat until the chutney is boiling hard and keep stirring to prevent it burning on the bottom.

The chutney is ready when it's only just looser than you'd like to eat it, is glossy with no visible liquid and a wooden spoon drawn along the bottom of the jam pan leaves a channel for a moment.

Ladle the chutney into the first jar, tap the jar on the work surface to encourage the chutney to settle, then gently burst any air bubbles with the knife, drawing it gently out of the jar after bursting them. Place the greaseproof circles on, if using, and twist on the lid.

Wipe down the jars and place on a cake rack to cool.

When cold label and store in a dark cupboard and ideally wait a couple of months before tasting.

Taste Test: 2 weeks later the hot chutney hasn't got hotter. Its heat is just warm, but it has become sweeter. I might add some ground ginger or cumin next time to give it a more earthy background flavour. This has kept well for a year.

Sloe & Apple Jelly

Wow! This jelly is a bit mad. It doesn't create foam on the surface, oh no, it creates a plasticky layer the colour of blancmange and the thickness of skin on cold custard. Maybe the layer is just a part of the berry that sets into a jelly before the rest, I just don't know.

I tried to skim it all off, but the stuff is so sticky I ended up using 5 spoons as I can't get the scum off the spoons and the stuff just keeps re-forming. I can't help but be amazed at the colour. The scum is just so completely different to the foamy scum you get off jam. If you skim too much when the jelly is still cooking you skim off too much actual jelly, so I stop skimming until after setting point has been reached. I tried dabbing the last bits off with unprinted kitchen towel (Internet advice) and this works, but it's even more faff.

JAMMY TIP

Given half a chance this will burn on the bottom of the jam pan, so after you've added the sugar and increased the heat, stir, stir and stir.

THE JAMMY BODGER

	Ingredients
No. of jars: 8 small jars, yielding about 1.9kg	1.8kg / 14½ cups apples (I used cooking apples, but eating apples are fine)
Time taken: 6 hours including the time taken to run it through the jelly bag twice	200g / 1⅓ cups sloes
	900ml / 3¾ cups water
	2kg / 10 cups granulated sugar (I got 3 pints of juice, so used 1.35 kg sugar)
	A squeeze of lemon juice or small sprinkle of vinegar to stop the apples going brown

Calculating Sugar Formula: 600ml / 2½ cups juice = 450g / 2¼ cups sugar

How to Make

Stage 1

You can just rinse your apples, but mine needed peeling, so peel the approximate amount of apples and place them in a bowl of water with a squeeze of lemon juice. Dice the apples into a bowl on the weighing scales so you can weigh them as you go. Add them to the jam pan.

Rinse and pick any stalks off the sloes, weigh and add to the jam pan with the water.

Bring the fruity water to the boil, then simmer until soft and pulpy (about 1 hour for the whole recipe, 30 minutes for a half measure) and mash with a potato masher if it needs help.

Scald the jelly bag and set up the jelly bowl and stand. When the fruit is pulpy, ladle it carefully into the jelly bag and leave it to drip through.

Stage 2 second straining (cooking or crab apples)

Leave the jelly bag to drip through until it has stopped dripping. If you feel motivated, turn the jelly bag contents back into the jam pan with just over 450ml / 1⅞cups of water and reheat until the fruit is hot and pulpy again.

Clean the jelly bag in hot soapy water, rinse well, then scald again and hang from the stand.

Ladle the fruity pulp into the jelly bag and leave to drip through again. You may have to empty the juice bowl into the measuring jug to make space for the second batch of juice in the bowl.

Clean the jam pan.

Stage 3

Prep your jars (cold oven 110°C / 225°F /Mk ¼ for 30 minutes) and lids, ladle and funnel (saucepan with boiling water for 20 seconds). Place 3 saucers in the fridge to test for set.

Measure all your juice and use the Calculating Sugar Formula beneath the Ingredients to work out how much sugar to add.

Pour the juice into the clean jam pan and, when warm, add the sugar and stir continuously until dissolved. Increase the heat and look to set the jelly.

When you are happy with the set, take the jam pan off the heat and start to skim off the thick layer of scum. Take your time as you have to get all the scum off as it will show in the jelly.

The scum must not be stirred in.

Ladle the jelly into small jars, twist the lids on tightly and place on a cake rack to cool.

Taste Test: If you hold a couple of these jars up to the light you can see a little pink blancmange worm against the ruby red of the jelly. This is because I stirred in the scum and consequently I'm not going to be able to sell them. I still feel strangely proud even though I have given birth to a worm, because I thought jelly making would be really hard.

The second batch of juice was much more watery, which is why you always have to mix both batches of juice, and meant the jelly took a while to reach setting point, so maybe it boiled off a lot of the second straining.

Steve's mum, Mary, uses equal quantities of cooking apples and sloes, adding just enough water to cover, and you can do a second boiling adding about half the amount of water. This jelly's flavour still has the astringency of the sloes, but it's not as tongue stripping as eating the berries straight from the bush.

Jelly Bag Empties

The amount of fruit left in the jelly bag is staggering, so I empty the jelly bag into a large pot and mulch through it with my hands to remove the stones. This takes a while, but as the 2nd jelly straining juice is bubbling away, this takes my mind off the pink scum that's forming. I used this as the fruity base for Eve's pudding and it would make a good fool stirred into custard, or it could be topped by crumble – basically the usual crew. This only works if you don't include the apple cores in the jelly, though.

Freezing

If you can, pick some extra sloes for freezing. If you know what you plan to use them for then simply rinse, weigh and bag them, labelling the bag with the weight and date frozen. If you're not sure, rinse, then lay the sloes on a tray in the freezer for an hour and then bag. This stops them sticking together, so when you defrost them you can just defrost the amount you need.

You can then make sloe and apple jelly later in the year, as different types of apples are available all winter, or you could freeze a batch for making into drunken berry jelly next January. You will need 2kg / 4lb 6oz blackberries and 500g / 1lb 2oz sloes frozen for this. You can buy frozen blackberries at the shops, but not sloes. I know what my freezer is full of... err... apples... but it will soon be full of sloes too.

Rosehips

Rosehips are very high in vitamin C, apparently as much as 20 times more than in oranges. During the 2nd World War hoards of British children were sent out picking them in order that a health giving syrup could be made and shared.

Rosehips bushes are a prickly nightmare. If a thorn catches your skin as you struggle to disentangle yourself, the thorn rips further into your flesh, leaving splinters in the skin and criss-cross lines that make you look like you've been self-mutilating.

You can pick rosehips when they are a deep red and you can get away with using them rock hard if you are chopping them up in the food processor, or wait a while until they are squidgy and chop them by hand.

Choose your picking companions wisely. A dog will not pick, a good friend like Delphine, will, and it's less demoralising than picking on your own. This particularly applies to making syrup, which takes a lot more picking.

You cook the apples first so that the rosehips only cook for a short time to preserve as much vitamin C as possible.

Be even more careful than usual that none drops directly into the bowl beneath when ladling rosehip mulch into the top of the jelly bag. If any rosehip bits get into the final jelly they can irritate your stomach. If they do drop in, empty the juice back into the jam pan and start ladling again.

Regula Guru wasn't surprised my hands itched as rosehips used to be the main component in itching powder!

Rosehip & Apple Jelly

After rinsing and de-tufting any dead heads and picking off any spikey stalks that might pierce the jelly bag, I attempted to chop the rosehips. Chopping rosehips is a nightmare. They are still really hard and bounce everywhere. Also, my hands are starting to itch and I'm feeling irritated as I'm losing a lot of rosehips on the floor. Why is it I feel I can rinse them after they've been outside and got who knows what on them, but if I drop one on the floor it has to go in the bin??

Don't rush to set the jelly. It had darkened in colour and was just staying apart on the saucer, so I whipped the jam pan off the heat and potted it as I didn't want to be late for work. Lo and behold, it didn't set properly (not at all, in actual fact). I couldn't face re-setting it, not that it's very hard, so I used it as a rosehip and apple cordial.

When you pour the fruity juice into the jam pan, leave the grainy bits at the bottom of the bowl.

Ingredients
650g / 2⅓ cups rosehips
1.5kg / 12 cups chopped apples (cookers or eaters not peeled or cored)
800ml / 3⅓ cups water
2kg / 10 cups sugar (this is more than enough)
Calculating Sugar Formula: 600ml / 2½ cups juice = 450g / 2¼ cups sugar

To make, follow the recipe for sloe and apple jelly or the basic guide to making jelly in the first section of the book.

Rosehip Syrup / Cordial

After 3 hours of picking and walking the haul is just over 2kg. I reassure Delphine I don't need any help making the syrup, as the picking was the hard part. How wrong can you be?

OK! The abbreviated version is it did not go according to plan. My swing top bottles' metal fastenings kept collapsing and when I tried to sterilise the bottles in a water bath in the jam pan, the water took over an hour to reach a boil and then covered the bottles inside and out with hard water scum. I reverted to sterilising the bottles in the oven.

Then when I tried to boil the rosehip syrup in a saucepan rather than my jam pan (it had the bottles in), it erupted like mount Vesuvius spewing a sea of molten orange liquid all over the hob top. When I was finally ready to bottle up the bottles were so hot I couldn't close them and once again their fastenings collapsed.

	Ingredients
No. of bottles (or jars): I've reduced the recipe, so it's much easier to cope with. With my 290ml bottles I'd need 5 or 6 as this recipe makes about 1.2 litres	**Ingredients**
	500g / 1⅞ cups rosehips
	400g / 2 cups granulated sugar (can vary from 250 -500g / 1¼-2½ cups, according to taste)
Time taken: 6 hours, including 3 hours watching the jelly bag dripping	1.5 litres / 6⅓ cups water
	1 tbsp lemon juice (optional, according to taste)

How to Make

Stage 1

Rinse and pick over the rosehips. Weigh and note the weight if it's different from the recipe and calculate the amount of water and sugar needed.

Bring 750ml / 1⅛ cups of water to the boil in the jam pan while mincing the rosehips in the food processor.

Add the rosehips to the boiling water and bring back to the boil, then take the jam pan off the heat and cover for 15 minutes to infuse.

Scald your jelly bag, hang it above the bowl, ladle in the rosehip liquid and leave to drain for 1 hour or until it only drips about once every 30 seconds.

Stage 2 second straining

Empty the jelly bag back into the jam pan and add 750ml / 1⅛ cups of boiling water from the kettle. Bring the mixture back to the boil, then remove from the heat, cover and infuse for 15 minutes again.

Rinse out the jelly bag, scald it again, then hang from the stand above the bowl. If the bowl is more than half full (you'll be lucky!), empty it into another jug or bowl so that there is enough space in the bowl for the next lot of juice.

Ladle the rosehip mixture into the jelly bag and leave to drip through for an hour or until it almost ceases.

Stage 3 preparing to bottle

Wash your jars or bottles and lids in hot soapy water, rinse, drain and prep in the oven.

If your funnel doesn't fit, sterilise a small jug in the oven along with your bottles / jars.

Empty the rosehips from the jelly bag into the composter, rinse out the bag, then leave in a bowl of boiling water and washing up liquid to rinse again later.

Pour all the rosehip juice into the clean jam pan, cauldron or stock pot, bring to a simmer and stir in the sugar, stirring continuously until dissolved.

Bring the syrup to the boil, then take off the heat. You can boil it for longer to reduce the syrup, but you may be destroying some of the vitamin C.

Either ladle through a funnel or pour into a measuring jug, then pour into bottles or jars up to 1cm / ⅓ inch from the top.

Taste Test: It's great drizzled on vanilla ice cream or into yoghurt. I prefer it mixed with cold milk, but I think that's the child in me. You can also freeze the syrup as ice cubes to drop into a drink.

Fruity Lessons Learnt / Things to Ponder

Small batches are best in terms of picking, preparing and expectations.

The syrup needs a big saucepan for enough space to boil vociferously and it is temperamental.

I also tried to heat process my bottles to make it keep longer, but it's a lot of faff. You can freeze the cordial in ice cube trays and when you want a drink, defrost an ice cube or add it to hot water. Or you could use a lot less water and make a really condensed syrup to save space, then freeze leaving space for expansion.

Fill the bottles up to 1cm from the top and you can sterilise as normal.

THE JAMMY BODGER

Oh my God!!!! I've stopped hyperventilating now! I tried to multiply the taste of autumn chutney recipe by three. I know I never learn. It took over 3 hours of non-stop chopping, then the pan was too full to boil down well enough, so I had to ladle some into a saucepan. Anyone else reminded of the blackcurrant jam?

I was getting a bit stressed by now. I was on a serious time constraint as I was putting 3 chickens to bed at 6pm, and then off to tap dancing.

As it was all taking too long, the cauldron that I'd put on to boil to sterilise the lids and spoons actually boiled dry and to prevent the fire alarm going off I popped the pot outside the window on the sill, making a mental note to remember it later. No, I didn't forget the pot. Just before I left I said to

myself 'Be careful' as I pulled the pot back into the flat...

...only I didn't pull the pot back into the flat. In my mind's eye I can see myself kind of pushing it out of the 3rd floor window and watching it fly through the air in slow motion and smash into the slate tiles of the 1st floor building's roof below, before clanging loudly onto the paving slabs beneath and spinning around. The noise was amazing; instinctively I ducked below the window sill.

What to do?? My heart is racing and I can hardly breathe. I phone Steve, cutting short his chirpy greeting with 'You won't believe what I've just done!' He knows I've got to confess or I will never forgive myself.

I steel myself and go to explain to the lady living

below. When she opens the door she is on the phone to her husband, possibly trying to work out how a cauldron had just landed in her garden. She was in fact holding the offending article. I explained, and she asked if I had insurance. I don't know what type of insurance would cover this, but I'm probably not covered.

When I pop around the next day with flowers (the least I could do), they both insist I take the pot back as it's a good pot, and find the tale amusing and don't want to take it further!!! Strangely they refuse my offer of chutney. What great people, and how lucky am I that the pot didn't hit either of them or the dog. All that's left now is to explain to the neighbours who came out to see what had created the awful racket. Although it's a great jam making story, it's going to have to remain a secret for now. Ssshhhh... (names have not been added to protect the innocent!)

I try to get back into the chutney making saddle, but my heart's not really in it. I think it best to finish with chutney making for this year.

Huckleberries are hip and happening... I have really got to get the jam pan back out as the huckleberries Regula planted out at The Vege Place are crying out to be picked. Garden huckleberries are a type of blueberry, but taste nothing like them. Hucks have a very strong and rather more savoury flavour. Lisalot (she's Swiss) thinks they have an aftertaste of cucumber, and a local restaurant is using them to accompany venison.

I used 1kg / 8 cups of apples to 2kg /13½ cups of hucks and 3kg / 15 cups of sugar, and used a potato masher to get the berry consistency I wanted. (Very strangely the slightly under-ripe berries had white seeds). Make half of this recipe if you have a standard jam pan.

It made 18 beautifully dark bluey / purple small jars (yielding approximately 4.3kg), and the flavour was good, although to Steve and I it had a slightly

menthol aftertaste. I had to be careful to get an equal quantity of liquid and fruit in each jar and I should probably have left it to stand for a couple of minutes and then stirred to get an even dispersal of fruit.

There are still loads of hucks left, so we are feeding some to the chickens to see if we get purple egg shells, or purple yolks. As yet they've had no effect.

Chutney tasting... We're off to Karma Colin's to sit around the fire and chill out as everyone has been running around like headless chickens (not the greatest phrase, as that is unfortunately what happened to Regula's chickens over the summer) lately, with the apple collecting, juicing, and delivery. It's my turn to cook and I'm feeling lazy and a bit unsure of my cooking abilities, so I take the chutneys and a random array of cheeses and chutneys and declare a Chutney Tasting Event.

It's a draw for first place between the Mediterranean Chutney and the Sweet 'n' Hot Pepper Jam, so obviously anything with peppers in is a favourite. Regula plumps for the Tongue Tingling Chutney, Steve nearly eats the whole jar of Sweet 'n' Hot Pepper Jam, and Karma Colin is left with an addiction to Mediterranean Chutney, which makes him easy to bribe. Regula's son Brian declares a love for toasted marshmallows, and refuses to try any, but you can't win them all! Nobody liked the Traditional Green Tomato Chutney, hence I've not included the recipe.

Quince Pastilles

The following quince pastille recipe is from local veg producer Regula who got it from her Auntie Margaret. The recipe doesn't use the quince juice, which could easily be made into a jelly:

Although we have a dry climate more suited to drying out fruit pastilles, I know Mel had a fair bit of trouble with them, but it's worth giving this recipe a go and drying them in a low oven.

500g quince pulp (or 750g-1kg fresh quinces)

400g sugar

2 tbsp lemon juice

To make quince pulp stew approximately 750g–1kg of fresh quinces in enough water to cover until soft and pulpy. Turn off the heat and leave to rest for a few hours.

Push the pulp through a nylon sieve, then weigh the pulp that's left in the sieve. Use the juice for quince jelly - it's the pulp we want here though.

Put the pulp, sugar and lemon juice into your jam pan and cook for 45 minutes, stirring continuously until it is so dry it actually comes away from the sides of the jam pan. This is a lot drier than a fruit butter! If you put a blob on a cold saucer after one minute you should be able to peel it off like plasticine, so stir frequently to prevent it catching on the bottom of the pan.

Sugar a large, flat baking tray and pour the mixture on so it's at most 1cm thick.

Leave to dry overnight in a very low oven, then cut into strips and store in an air tight jar or biscuit tin.

NOVEMBER

Princely Poppadom Pumpkin Chutney

No. of jars: 7 small densely packed jars, about 1.7kg.	**Ingredients**
Time taken: 1 hour prep, 1 hour simmering, 1½ hours simmer after the sugar was added and 20 minutes to pot	900g / 7¾ cups cubed pumpkin or butternut squash
	3 onions finely sliced
	225g / 2 cups cooking apples, peeled and cubed
	225g / 2 cups marrow
	50g / ⅓ cup dates (ready to eat – chopped, no stones)
	450ml / 2 cups cider vinegar
	1 tbsp each of curry powder, ground turmeric, ground cumin, ground ginger, ground coriander, cardamom seeds (amount after de-podding, or 1tbsp in a spice bag)
	450g / 2¼ cups granulated sugar
	2 cloves garlic, crushed.
	3 dried chillies finely sliced
	1 tbsp light oil

How to Make

Prep and weigh your squash or pumpkin, onions, chillies, garlic, apples, marrow and dates, and measure out your vinegar ready for action.

Gently bash the cardamom pods in the pestle and mortar to release their seeds, discard the shell, add the other whole spices and continue bashing until as finely ground as possible. Add the other spices and mix, or put all the spices in a spice bag

Warm the oil in the bottom of your stock pot or jam pan, add the spices and after 1 minute add the garlic and chillies. You want them to simmer gently in the oil, not burn.

Add the onion mix to coat in the spices and fry for about 10 minutes until softened. Add a couple of tablespoons of water and reduce the heat if it's starting to stick or burn.

Add all your veg, the apples and dates, and stir to combine with the spices, then add the vinegar and mix well.

Bring the chutney to the boil, reduce the heat and simmer for 45 minutes or until the vegetables are soft, but with a little bite, stirring occasionally. Check by tasting the hardest veg, for me that's the carrots.

Add the sugar and stir until it has completely dissolved, then simmer gently for 1 hour until the liquid has been absorbed / the chutney is glossy / or if you scrape your wooden spoon along the bottom of the pan it leaves a trail. Stir continuously, taking care that the chutney does not burn on the bottom.

Prep your jars (cold oven 110°C / 225°F / Mk ¼ for 30 minutes) and lids, ladle, funnel and bubble bursting knife (saucepan with boiling water for 20 seconds). Prepare some greaseproof circles if you aren't sure your lids are vinegar-proof.

If your chutney still has a lot of water to boil off after 45 minutes of simmering, increase the heat but stir frequently to prevent burning.

When ladling your chutney into the jars, tap them on the work surface to encourage the chutney to settle, then use the knife to pierce any air bubbles. Remember the chutney will shrink back slightly, so don't be stingy.

Screw your lids on tightly (greaseproof paper before the lids, if using), and when cold, label and store for at least a month before trying. It will keep for up to a year.

Taste Test: Sweet with a vinegary edge, but not too much. This has the best texture and like the farmhouse pickle I've simmered it down so that it's thick, but each piece of veg is separate – some chutney's sadly end up all of a mush.

THE JAMMY BODGER
Herby Apple Jelly

I've still got loads of eating apples sitting around looking at me petulantly and telling me off for the waste. They've started to produce their own wax now, like the fake wax finish in the shop, as if saying look I'm doing my bit, just use me! Hmm... what about a herby jelly to go with a roast or fish, or to baste a joint of meat for the last ten minutes. I'm not sure how well it will work out with eating apples, but hopefully the herby happenings will take over.

Dampen your herbs beforehand in a sieve, then when you add them to the jelly they will sink as opposed to floating on the surface.

No. of jars: 4½ medium jars, yielding about 1.5kg	Ingredients
Time taken: 1 hour prep, 1 hour simmering down, then leave to drip through and then 1½ hours sorting it out	First Stage:
	1.5 kg / 12 cups apples, roughly chopped
	900ml / 3¾ cups water
Cooking or crab apples add a much better flavour and if your apples are particularly sour, add only half the vinegar	6-8 large sprigs fresh herbs (rosemary or sage)
	300ml / 1¼ cups white vinegar / distilled malt vinegar /white wine vinegar / apple cider vinegar
	Second stage:
	5 tbsp fresh herbs, finely chopped (rosemary or sage)
	Juice of 1 lemon

Calculating Sugar Formula: 600ml / 2½ cups juice = 450g / 2¼ cups sugar

NB. Make sure to remove the large herb sprigs before pouring the apple mush into the jelly bag as they might tear the bag.

If your herbs rise to the surface in the jars after potting, shake the jars every now and then and as the jelly starts to set it will hold them in place.

How to Make

Stage 1

Apples: weigh, rinse, scratch over, then top and tail to remove any muddy bits. Chop and place in the jam pan with the water and large sprigs of herbs (if you've only got smaller sprigs, tie them into a bundle or pop in a muslin bag so they are easy to remove later).

Bring the apple mulch to the boil, then reduce the heat to simmer gently until really soft.

When soft, remove the herbs, add the vinegar and mash with a potato masher or the back of a wooden spoon to make the apples really pulpy.

Scald your jelly bag and set up the jelly bag and stand.

Ladle the apple mush into the jelly bag and leave to strain through until it stops dripping (about 5 or 6 hours), or overnight.

Stage 2

Prep your jars (cold oven 110°C / 225°F / Mk ¼ for 30 minutes) and lids, ladle and funnel (saucepan with boiling water for 20 seconds). Place 3 saucers in the fridge to test for set.

Pour the apple juice into a measuring jug, note the volume, then pour into your clean jam pan.

Work out how much sugar you need.

Warm the juice until simmering gently, then pour in the sugar, add the lemon juice and stir continuously until dissolved.

Increase the heat, stop stirring and look to set the jelly. This should take about 10 minutes after it really starts to boil. When you are happy it has set, go to the next stage.

Stage 3

Remove the jam pan from the heat and leave to stand for 5 minutes, then skim off any scum.

Finely chop your herbs, then dampen them with cold water in a sieve and add to the jelly.

Leave the jelly to stand for another 5 minutes until it starts to thicken, then stir in the herbs and ladle the jelly into the jars, twisting the lids on tightly.

Taste Test: Leave for a couple of days before tasting. It's herby and flavoursome, but if you'd rather have a totally clear jelly then you don't need to add any of the herbs at the end as the flavour will already have permeated fully, and the jelly should taste as strong as the sprigs of herb you have used.

THE JAMMY BODGER

Farmhouse Chutney

I'm trying to make a savoury all round people pleaser, so fingers crossed.

No. of jars: 6 medium, about 750g yield	Ingredients
Time taken: 45 minutes prep, 2½ hours cooking down, and 15 minutes pot ting = 3hours in total	500g / 1lb 2oz carrots, small cauliflower florets, a swede or turnips, peeled and diced
You can play around with the ingredients depending on what you've got, as long as the overall weight remains the same	350g / 3 medium onions, finely sliced
	225g / 2 medium cooking apples, peeled and diced
	250g / 2¼ cups marrow (winter squash), peeled and de-seeded
	150g / 1 cup (packed) dates or raisins (I think you know which I added)
	8 cloves

 You might need to get a larger compost caddy as there's loads of leftovers from this.

How to Make

Dice all the veg, thinly slice the onions, then add all the spices and vinegar and everything else to the jam pan. Bring slowly to the boil.

Simmer until all the veg is soft – the carrots will probably take longest. If the vegetables don't seem to be softening after an hour or so, cover the pan to increase the temperature within, but without burning the veg on the bottom. Keep an eye on it.

Prep your jars (cold oven 110°C / 225°F / Mk ¼ for 30 minutes) and lids, ladle, funnel and bubble bursting knife (saucepan with boiling water for 20 seconds). Prep your greaseproof circles too, if using.

Your chutney is ready when the liquid has evaporated and it looks glossy and thick, or if you draw a spoon across the bottom of the pan and it leaves a tail.

Ladle some into the first jar, tapping it on the work surface to help it settle, and using the knife to burst any large air bubbles. Withdraw the knife slowly and after all the air bubbles are burst, place on a greaseproof cicle, if using, and twist the lid on tightly. Then move on to the next jar.

Fill all the jars in this way and leave on a cake rack to cool.

Taste Test: Everyone likes this. It's good and traditional and of course it's great with cheddar cheese. If I'm aiming to please people I must try and make piccalilli too next year, but I'm scared by the traditional fluorescent yellow colouring.

Monkey's Bottom... Open-Arse... I'm actually talking medlars. You can imagine how delightful the fruit is from its numerous unpleasant nicknames. You can't believe how strange they look - even the birds don't touch them. That said, I was really excited to find that nearby Godlingston Manor Farm has a medlar tree that is collapsing under the weight of this old fashioned fruit, and I can't wait to see what they taste like.

Picking the medlars was made more challenging by the interest of Henry, a hand reared calf who showed his enthusiasm by head-butting Regula repeatedly - obviously a sign of affection - until Ben, whose farm it is, encouraged Henry to leave by getting him to chase him. Henry can be seen on YouTube by entering 'new born calf henry.' Although he is bigger now, he's still very cute.

Medlars have to be 'bletted' before they are even edible. I'm not sure whether bletted means left to rot or left to ripen, but either way after 2 weeks stored in a cardboard box with newspaper dividing layers, some of the fruit are sweaty and mouldy, some haven't ripened at all, and some are squishy and oozing a dark sticky stuff. When I eventually make myself taste one, they taste kind of like caramelised apple with a date-like twang.

Medlar Jelly

Ingredients
2.2kg / 4lb 14oz medlars, chopped
2.3 litres / 9¾ cups water (use less if most of the medlars are ripe 'n' squishy)
2kg / 10 cups granulated sugar (more than enough)
Juice of 1 medium sized lemon
Calculating Sugar Formula: 600ml / 2½ cups juice = 450g / 2¼ cups sugar. If the fruit is very ripe, add 2 tbsp extra lemon juice

THE JAMMY BODGER

How to Make

Stage 1

There is no need to peel or remove the seeds of medlars and you couldn't anyway. Simply rinse and pick over (pretty tough in itself), then weigh, add to the jam pan and squidge them up with your hands before heating. It's one way to get to know your fruit intimately!

Add enough water to cover and bring to the boil. Reduce the heat and simmer for about 1 hour until the fruit is completely pulpy.

Scald the jelly bag and ladle the fruity mulch into the jelly bag and leave to drip through overnight.

Stage 2

Prep your jars (cold oven 110°C / 225°F / Mk ¼ for 30 minutes) and lids, ladle and funnel (saucepan with boiling water for 20 seconds). Place 3 saucers in the fridge to test for set.

Empty the jelly bag (keep the mulch if you are making fruit cheese) and pour the juice from the bowl into the measuring jug.

Work out how much sugar you need.

Warm the juice in the jam pan, then add the sugar and lemon juice, stirring continuously until the sugar has dissolved. Then bring to a rapid boil until setting point is reached (which can take a while).

When you are happy with the set, ladle into jars.

Taste Test: The jelly has real depth of flavour, although I can't quite put my finger on what that flavour is; is it caramelised apple or apple cooked with date? Somehow it reminds me more of a savoury pudding. Although not very tart it is good with roast meats or on muffins. It's an adult sweet tooth fix. I wish I could describe it better, but at least now you will have to make it to find out.

Some Medlar Jelly Thoughts

Store your medlar jelly somewhere cool and dark.

Initially I stuck to the minimum amount of water, although I could tell it wasn't enough. About 4 drips came out of the jelly bag, and I won't even describe what the thick, dark brown stuff in the jelly bag looked like! I had to turn out the mulch back into the jam pan and reheat with another 1.2 litres of water. Lesson learnt – if it looks too thick to drip, it probably is.

Sloe Gin

We filled an old vinegar bottle with about **500g / 3⅓cups of sloes**, which had been pierced, and then added about **125g / ⅔cup of sugar**, and shook the bottle to mix. The rest of the bottle was filled with **cheap gin**, nearly to the top. This was then given a shake and placed in a dark cupboard where it was given an occasional shake until it was ready to be transferred to a prettier bottle as a Christmas present for my brother. If the berries have been pierced well enough they will be edible later, as they will lose some of their astringent bitterness.

Medlar Fruit Butter

No. of jars: 3 jars (at a guess – it works out different each time) Time taken: 1 hour to push through the sieve, 1 hour to thicken in the jam pan	Ingredients 2kg / 4lb 8oz medlars 2kg / 10 cups granulated sugar Juice of 1 large lemon Enough water to cover
Calculating Fruit Butter Sugar: 600ml / 2½ cups juice = 450g / 2¼ cups sugar	

How to Make

Place the medlars in the pan with enough water to cover. Mulch them with a potato masher, bring to the boil, then reduce to a simmer until pulpy and thick like lumpy custard.

Push your lumpy 'custard' through a sieve.

Pour your medlar juice into a measuring jug and note the amount of sugar you will need using the sugar calculation.

Warm the juice in the pan, then add the sugar, stirring continuously until the sugar dissolves. Add the lemon juice.

Prep your jars (cold oven 110°C / 225°F / Mk ¼ for 30 minutes) and lids, ladle and funnel (saucepan with boiling water for 20 seconds). Place 3 saucers in the fridge to test for set.

Stir occassionally until the mixture starts to thicken, then stir continuously until it's like a thick cheese sauce. If you drop a small blob on a cold saucer it should hold together.

Pour into jars and twist on the lids.

DECEMBER

THE JAMMY BODGER
Sloe & Apple Jelly

There were so many sloes around this year that I couldn't make full use of the glut, so I rinsed, weighed, bagged and froze them. Now is a great time to bash out a few jellies for Christmas using a recipe of equal apples to equal sloes. (For the full recipe check out Sloe and Apple Jelly in October.)

I defrosted **1.9kg of sloes / 12.75 cups** overnight and peeled and chopped **1.9 kg / 15¼ cups of eating apples**. I peeled the apples as they've been sitting around a bit and have started creating their own waxy sheen. I mulched in them in the jam pan with **1.8 litres / 7½ cups of water** for about 3 hours (I was pottering around and didn't really notice the time). With this quantity you really need 2 separate jelly bags and stands, so if you haven't got two, use half the amount of fruit. They took 4 hours to drip through, and I got **2.4 litres /10 cups of juice**, so I added **1.8kg / 9 cups of sugar**, followed by **the juice of 2 lemons**.

As I marvelled at the fab colour, suddenly it dawned on me that time was ticking by and the jelly wasn't setting. I hadn't heeded by own advice and allowed an **extra 10% of sloes** as they were frozen, and between them and my tired apples there wasn't enough pectin to set the jelly. Realising the error of my ways I chucked in **140ml / ½ cup of home-made apple pectin stock** which had been waiting unloved in the fridge for a couple of weeks. Thankfully the jelly saw the error of its ways and set. I made only 9 medium and 1 small jar, or 3.2kg even with the double jelly bag action.

Taste Test: It's still the tartest berry jelly yet.

Oh cranberry, where art thou hiding? There are loads of cranberry jelly recipes, so I assumed cranberries, which are in season from November, were abundant here and would be readily available in the run up to Christmas. I assumed wrong. It turns out cranberries used to be prolific in East Anglia, but since the fens were drained they are usually imported from America, so are never going to be readily available here other than dried.

Next year I'm going to freeze redcurrants to use instead. I think you could use dried cranberries, using them like dried apricots ie. soaked for a few hours and then cooked in their soaking liquid, but at this time of year my brain's not up to the faff of playing with recipes. Next step - where the hell am I going to get hold of star anise?

JAMMY TIP

Respect frozen fruit. It does its best, but its pectin is just not up to scratch. If possible have some home-made pectin stock and/or lemons to hand in busy periods, or keep some pectin sachets or a bottle of unopened liquid pectin in the cupboard.

Mulled Red Jelly

I made it twice, but both times I ended up with scum suspended throughout the jelly and a funny set. Then I realised my mistake! I had thought cranberries were high pectin and recipes said you could use frozen or fresh with no change in the amount of fruit, so assumed I could do a second straining and didn't need to add pectin. It turns out they are more medium pectin than high, so when frozen would become low pectin, and even lower with a second straining. Taking the above into account it's 3rd time lucky, and it set beautifully.

No. of jars: 4 medium jars, yielding about 1.3kg with no second straining	Ingredients
Time taken: 2hours not including dripping	1.2kg / 12 cups cranberries / redcurrants / sloes frozen (OR 1.1kg / 11cups fresh)
	1 cinnamon stick broken in half
	4 or 5 star anise
	1 tbsp whole cloves
Have a lemon handy in case yours struggles to set. I'm reluctant to add this in the ingredients as the jelly should (SHOULD!) set without it	1 dried chilli
	700ml / 3 cups water
	2kg / 10 cups granulated sugar
	150ml / ⅔ cup full bodied red wine (optional)
	Juice of 1 lemon

Calculating Sugar Formula: 600ml / 2½ cups juice = 450g / 2¼ cups sugar

How to Make

Stage 1

Put everything except the sugar and wine into the jam pan and bring to the boil.

Cover, reduce the heat and simmer gently for 15 minutes or until the cranberries are completely mushy. Squeeze them with the back of the wooden spoon to make them burst.

Scald the jelly bag, then hang from the jelly stand and ladle the fruit mulch into the jelly bag, leaving it to strain through for about 4 hours or until it stops dripping.

Stage 2 – second straining (optional, and only with fresh fruit)

Empty the jelly bag back into the clean jam pan and add 400-500ml / 1⅔-2⅛ cups of water; enough to be able to mulch the fruit again. Bring to the boil then simmer gently uncovered for 10 minutes.

Wash your jelly bag in hot soapy water, rinse, then scald again and hang from the stand.

Ladle the fruity pulp into the jelly bag and leave to drip through overnight.

Stage 3

Prep your jars (cold oven 110°C / 225°F / Mk ¼ for 30 minutes) and lids, ladle and funnel (saucepan with boiling water for 20 seconds). Place 3 saucers in the fridge to test for set.

Empty the juice into a measuring jug, note the amount of juice, then pour into the jam pan and warm gently.

Work out the sugar required and add to the jam pan, stirring continuously until dissolved.

THE JAMMY BODGER

Add the wine, increase the heat and look to set.

When you are happy with the set, skim off all the scum, taking your time as there will be a lot. Finally, ladle into jars.

Taste Test: Really tart, fruity and warming with the spices; great with meat or with a cheese smorgåsbord (I just wanted to use that word), which is why, despite my struggles, I would make it again with redcurrants, and I'm still eating it even with the scum in.

Variations: Add orange zest and a couple of tbsp of the juice to the jelly juice after straining.

Use a frozen mix of berries and currants and try to make sure there are some tart berries in the mix. I used 2 x 450g packs of mixed berries and currants.

You actually get about 400g of fruit in each pack, so I topped up the weight with cranberries. If you've mainly got soft berries you might need to reduce the water, so start with just 400ml / 1⅔ cups, and see if it's got enough water to mulch down. If it hasn't then top it up bit by bit to 750ml / 3⅛ cups. I needed the full amount.

If your fruit is frozen you definitely need to add lemon juice as this jelly wavered before deciding to set, suspended scum and all.

You could just add a tbsp of booze and stir it in at the end. Karma Colin stirs this into hot water for a tangy winter cordial. I forgot to tell him he's got the really boozy one. He's just asked me for a 2nd jar.

Gooseberry & Elderberry Jam (frozen)

I'm a bit gutted I didn't make this before the market as several people asked for a gooseberry jam, and who can blame them. I defrosted **1kg / 6½ cups of gooseberries**, and **100g / ⅔ cup of elderberries** that I had frozen over the summer. I warmed and squidged the berries with **300ml / 1¼ cups of water** until the fruit skins were soft. Then I added **900g / 4½ cups of sugar**, reasoning that as this recipe was originally for 900g and the extra 100g is to offset the loss of pectin, then the amount of sugar should be the same as that of viable fruit. I hope you followed all that.

Add up to **200g / 1cup more sugar** if you prefer a sweeter jam, or if your gooseberries are particularly tart. I stirred until dissolved then increased the heat to set to the jam. I had **½ a lemon juiced** in case I needed it, but I didn't. What an easy jam to set, and what a great flavour. You can still see the elderberries in it, and it looks polka dotted.

Clementines in Brandy

I first made this with granulated sugar, but the clementines looked like they were floating in wee, so I hotfooted it to the shops to get Demerara sugar which looks loads better. Once again you need short, fat jars as otherwise it's a struggle to fit even 3 clementines in and it looks a bit stingy.

No. of jars: 4 large jars or about 1.5 litres	Ingredients
Time taken: 1 hour, and most of that spent peeling clementines	350g / 1½ cups (packed) Demerara Sugar
	600ml / 2½ cups brandy or cointreau
	750-800g (about 10-15) clementines
	250ml / 1 cup water
	4 cinnamon sticks, one for each jar you are using
	4 dried bay leaves, again one for each jar

How to Make

Prep your jars (cold oven 110°C / 225°F / Mk ¼ for 30 minutes) and lids, ladle and funnel (saucepan with boiling water for 20 seconds).

Peel the clementines, removing as much pith as possible and pierce them a few times each with a cocktail stick or fork.

Dissolve the sugar in the water in a medium sized saucepan over a medium heat, stirring continuously.

Remove the jars from the oven and pack the clementines in as tightly as possible, pushing them down and around a bit with the tongs, and add 1 bay leaf and 1 cinnamon stick to each jar.

Remove the syrup saucepan from the heat and add 500ml of the brandy.

Pour the brandy syrup into a jug and pour over the clementines, filling the jars right to the top. The extra 100ml of brandy is in case the jars need a top up – if you haven't enough syrup, top up with brandy.

Twist the lids on tightly and store in a dark cupboard for at least a month before eating.

This keeps for 12 months

Taste Test: Regula Guru had warned me that the clementines hadn't absorbed the brandy, but when I tasted them it was my turn to spit something straight back out. I don't like pure brandy. I spoke to Julia in the fish shop and she agreed that the clementines haven't been juicy this year, but the main problem was there wasn't enough sugar to prevent the brandy from blowing my tongue to pieces. I have amended the recipe with this in mind, and hope to have better luck next year, as floating clementines do look good – I just need to make them taste good.

Figs in Earl Grey à la Delphine Fawke

Ingredients	
300g / 2 cups dried figs	200ml / ⅞ cup cider vinegar
2 onions, red if preferred	½ tsp ground ginger
1 tbsp sunflower oil	¼ tsp grated nutmeg
150g / ¾ cup caster sugar	2 cloves
200ml / ⅞ cup cider vinegar	1 Earl Grey tea bag
	Salt and pepper

How to Make

Rinse and trim your figs, then leave to dry slightly. Soak the tea bag in 300ml of boiling water, then remove and soak the figs in the tea for 20 minutes.

Prep your jars (cold oven 110°C / 225°F / Mk ¼ for 30 minutes) and lids, ladle and funnel (saucepan with boiling water for 20 seconds).

Take the figs out of the tea and cut into small pieces.

Dice the onions finely and fry gently in the oil for 3 minutes until softened.

Add 3 tbsp of the tea and simmer for another 10 minutes.

Add the sugar and stir to dissolve, then add the figs and simmer for 5 minutes.

Add the vinegar and all the spices and cook on a low heat for 1 hour, stirring occasionally and more often when it starts to thicken.

Remove the cloves, pour into the sterilised pots and twist the lids on tightly.

Candied Peel

When using peel you really need to have faith in your fruit. Hopefully it's not been sprayed with a load of rubbish and covered in a thick waxy finish. If you're not sure, get the best fruit you can, preferably organic, and give it a really good scrub, scratching off any discoloured or marked sections.

It's good to use a range of fruit with a variety of different coloured peels, which is why it's handy to get either limes or a pomelo (a Chinese grapefruit – I didn't know what it was either) to add to the mix. Although when I struggled to balance the pomelo to score and slice the skin, suddenly the large, unwieldy fruit didn't seem such a good idea.

Handy hint: You will need two large baking trays, lined with greaseproof paper to lay the peel out on to dry and somewhere to leave the peel where it won't get things spilt on it. If you really can't find anywhere, dry the peel for about 6 hours or overnight in a really low oven.

	Ingredients
No. of jars: 3 medium jars. It will look prettier in smaller jars and you'll feel like you've got more.	**Ingredients**
	2 oranges, 1 grapefruit, and 1 pomelo (probaby the equivalent of 2 fruit)
Time taken: 20 minutes prep, 1½ hours simmering, 20 minutes slicing, 24 hours to dry and then 15 minutes sugaring	500g / 2½ cups granulated sugar
	Caster sugar for coating, or extra granulated

How to Make

Stage 1

Score the surface of each fruit into quarters, then pull the peel off by nudging it with your thumb whilst pulling gently. Take your time scraping the pith away from the peel with a small sharp knife, because if the peel isn't thin enough it won't dry and will be chewy. If the peel rips, don't worry, just slice it cleanly where the tear is. I was really pleased with this; it looked like it should and went according to plan for a change.

Weigh the peel. This is the weight of sugar you will need.

Place the peel in a large saucepan with enough water to cover and simmer gently for 1-1½ hours until the peel is soft. Change the water 3 times, each time returning to a simmer.

Drain the peel in a colander and scrape out the inner pulp, leaving the peel quite thin. Cut the peel into the shape of your choice, but leaving them large enough to pick up with tongs.

Place the peel and its equal weight in granulated sugar in a tightly fitting saucepan. You may need to use a smaller pan and barely cover with water. Bring to the boil then simmer very gently for 45 minutes or until the peel is translucent and has absorbed nearly all the syrup. I had just about 200ml left.

THE JAMMY BODGER

Using tongs lay the peel on baking trays lined with baking / greaseproof paper, and leave in a warm room for 24 hours or longer to dry out. Mine took 2 days, but it wasn't very warm.

Stage 2

Sterilise your jars in the oven for 30 minutes and your lids in a saucepan of boiling water for 20 seconds, then drain. Make sure the lids are dry before you use them.

Place some caster sugar in a small bowl and thoroughly coat each piece of peel before placing it in the jam jar. When full, twist the lid on tightly and store in a cool dark cupboard for up to 6 months.

Taste Test: I tasted some fancy shop-bought candied peel the week before; big thick wedges of peel which hadn't had their innards scraped out and I found it inedible. The normal supermarket variety don't even taste of fruit. Although candied peel is a weird thing to eat a slice of as it's still got the bitterness of the rind, this tasted so much better, and when shredded on the top of an iced cake will taste even better. Next time I would dry it a little bit more, maybe leaving it for another day.

As there is so much fruit left after making this I couldn't resist making a citrusy curd (or I could have used the juice mixed with icing sugar on a drizzle cake). I warmed the fruit segments with enough water not to stick, then pressed them through a sieve. Then I followed the method for making lemon curd in February using 3 eggs, 150g / ⅔ cup (1⅓ sticks) of butter, and 450g / 2¼ cups of sugar. It made a very rich, buttery curd. I think less butter and 1 more egg would perhaps have been even better, but I still felt pleased with myself as the fruit wasn't wasted.

Christmas Market

This year has been a big enough learning curve as it is, so I haven't focused on selling, but after a stock take it suddenly seems like a good idea as I've got more than enough, and there are only so many you can give away for Christmas.

I've been really lucky as my market stall has simply organised itself. I've ended up not part of the official market as I couldn't get a stall, but Running Shop Roger has lent me a table and I've set up outside the florist, who are of course both thanked with jam.

Customers seem happier to browse and buy more if you are standing chatting with a mate, so your full attention is not on them. But nobody buys anything from a bearded man dressed head to toe in black who won't meet their eye, so it was a good job I didn't leave Steve on the stall for long.

Once again I sold out of traditional sounding chutneys such as 'Winter Warmer,' whereas 'Gutsy Green Tomato' is coming home with me. Once again I realise jellies need to be renamed as jam, as they looked great, and I said they tasted great, but they still didn't sell. Several people asked if you could use it like jam. YES, YES, YES!

I feel really positive as I didn't set any sales targets for the market stall, or even for this year, so there was no pressure. I think it makes sense to concentrate my first year on the produce, as that takes enough time and effort in itself. I'm telling this to Steve as he looks at my negative balance sheet. There is the distinct possibility he will think I should focus more on selling.

PS. Happy Christmas and New Year.

JANUARY

Not Making Marmalade: Everyone, from old grannies to the man in the pharmacy is chatting about making marmalade. It must be Seville orange time, but why the fuss; they're only oranges? I'm telling anyone who will listen that I'm not making marmalade as I'd rather stick to home grown fruit.

But I'm being a hypocrite as I use loads of lemons and they are hardly grown in Dorset. I begrudge the supermarket price, so I've got 5kg of luscious lemons from Somerset Organic Link (over the border) stored in a cool box, bought especially for the purpose, with layers of newspaper in between them. I haven't put the ice packs in as I think they will make everything damp when they defrost. The cool box is stored in the cupboard in our hallway as it's cool and dark, and fingers crossed the lemons will live happily ever after - well until it's time for the chop at least. Hence lots of lemon recipes to follow.

Lemony Lemon Curd

I love lemon curd, and the lemonier the better. Organic lemons are best as you use the zest in the curd and you don't want to have to worry about what's been sprayed on their skin. It's usually easy to get hold of organic lemons, but if you can't you need to give your lemons a really good scrub, and if they've been waxed, scrub them with sugar and then rinse. To make the most of your lemons, encourage them to release more juice by pressing and rolling them across a table or work surface.

You can play with the recipe to suit your taste; use 4 lemons rather than 3 for a lemony twang, or if you prefer a sweeter curd and want it to keep for up to 4 months, add 450g / 2¼ cups of sugar, or add more butter and eggs or egg yolks for extra creaminess and thickness. I've added too much lemon juice before now in search of a hard hitting lemony twang, and was left with a runny curd. If you want to increase the

THE JAMMY BODGER

twang even more than 4 lemons, add zest rather than juice, and in the event of a runny curd emergency, add an extra egg yolk. If it's too late you can still save the curd by sticking it in the fridge to thicken.

No. of jars: 2 medium jars yielding about 650g, but this is enough as this curd only keeps for 2 months. Time taken: 2 hours	Ingredients 3 or 4 large lemons (preferably organic and unwaxed) 4 medium eggs 225g / 1⅛ cups caster sugar 115g / 1 stick butter

How to Make

Prep your jars (cold oven 110°C / 225°F / Mk ¼ for 30 minutes) and lids, ladle and funnel (saucepan with boiling water for 20 seconds).

Rinse, scrub if necessary, then zest the lemons into a large heatproof mixing bowl. You only want the very yellow outside, not the white pith as this will make the curd bitter.

Halve the lemons, then juice and sieve the juice into the bowl, probably about 9-12 tbsp of juice.

Add the sugar and roughly cubed butter to the bowl and place the bowl over a saucepan of simmering water, bain marie style.

Whisk or stir briskly until the butter has melted.

Whisk the eggs in a small bowl and, taking the curd bowl off the heat, sieve in the eggs. Rub the eggs through the sieve with a spoon, then scrape the bottom of the sieve to remove any egg that's clinging on.

Whisking and sieving the eggs prevents stringy bits in the curd.

Return the curd bowl to the saucepan and stir or whisk occasionally until thick, then stir continuously, particularly scraping around the edge of the bowl.

Occasionally check the water in the saucepan in case it starts to boil rapidly, or isn't simmering as hard as is needed to thicken the curd.

When the curd has thickened enough to coat the back of a wooden spoon (usually about 20 minutes after adding the egg), it is done. It will thicken slightly more when cooled.

Ladle into warm jars and twist the lids on tightly.

Label when cold and place somewhere cool and dark, or just start eating and then keep in the fridge. Whatever you do don't put them in the cupboard and forget about them as they only keep for a couple of months.

Taste Test: Fabulously zesty and lighter than shop-bought, with none of the claggy aftertaste. Great stirred into whipped cream or crème fraiche and meringue. Regula Guru ate a whole jar at one sitting, but that's what comes of doing lots of physically exhausting outdoor work.

Variations: Try using limes in the recipe above, or for a zingy version use **6 limes** and **350g / 1¾ cups of sugar**, with the rest of the ingredients the same.

Try orange and lemon curd using **2 oranges** and **2 lemons** in the same lemon curd recipe.

Apple Custard Curd

Peel and dice **3 large cooking apples**, then soften in approximately **100ml / ½ cup water**. Cook gently until soft and fluffy, then beat with a wooden spoon to a thick purée. Then continue as per the curd recipe, adding **2 lemons, 125g / ½ cup (1 stick) butter**, roughly cubed, **450g / 2¼ cups granulated sugar** and **5 or 6 medium eggs**.

Everyone is still talking about marmalade, so I bite the bullet and give it a go. It turns out there's a lot to learn about marmalade, so please don't be put off by some of the upcoming marmalade disasters. I'm now approaching marmalade with the level of reverence it deserves and we are now getting along famously. All the recipes have been modified, some with a News Flash to avoid the obvious elephant traps that I blundered into (err... several times), and a few I managed to create for myself.

Lemon & Ginger Marmalade

Despite all my care in slicing the lemons a few pips rose to the surface, so look out for them and scoop them out. Setting point was quite difficult to tell as the marmalade wasn't quite staying separate on the saucer, but it was definitely doing the 'I'm setting' boil. I dipped a metal spoon in and turned it on its side and bits congealed on the back, so I thought, 'That's good enough for me. It's a miracle, I can recognise setting point – this marmalade business is easy.' I spoke too soon, of course, and the marmalade had to be reset with two jam jars full of water. It reset really quickly, so I reassured myself it must have just been on the cusp of setting first time around. In fact it reset like a rock.

	Ingredients
No. of jars: 5 medium jars, and the yield should be about. 1.6kg	1.2kg / 2lb 10oz unwaxed lemons, preferably organic (about 10)
Time taken: Prep 1¾ hours (including a 30 minute trip to the shop for more ginger), then 2 hours simmering and 20 minutes setting, so about 4½ hours not including re-setting	100g / 3½ oz root ginger (2 medium knobs), or use a cheat's version
	1.2 litres / 5 cups water
	1kg / 5 cups granulated sugar

How to Make

Stage 1

Weigh the lemons, scrub and rinse, scrubbing with sugar if they are waxed. Halve and juice them.

Quarter the lemons, scrape out and chop up any pulp, and add it all to the jam pan. Put any really thick bits of pith into a small bowl for later.

Slice the peel thinly, taking your time. Flick the pips into the small bowl.

Add the peel to the jam pan and then add the water.

Peel, roughly chop and bash the ginger to help release the flavour, then add it to the small bowl.

Tip the contents of the small bowl into a piece of muslin, tie it up tightly with string and add to the jam pan.

News flash: At the end of stage 1 leave the pre-marmalade to soak for a couple of hours or overnight to start softening the peel.

THE JAMMY BODGER

Stage 2

Bring the marmalade to the boil, reduce the heat, cover with a lid and simmer for about 2 hours or until the peel is really tender. Taste it to check.

Remove the muslin bag, let it cool, then squeeze it out over the jam pan to release the juices.

Prep your jars (cold oven 110°C / 225°F / Mk ¼ for 30 minutes) and lids, ladle and funnel (saucepan with boiling water for 20 seconds). Place 3 saucers in the fridge to test for set.

Weigh the sugar and stir into the simmering marmalade over a low heat and keep stirring until it has completely dissolved.

Increase the heat and bring the marmalade to

setting point. You are looking for a fast, continuous boil where it boils all over the surface and makes a 'put, put, put' noise. The boil should be constant and doesn't rise up the jam pan. As soon as you think it's set, whip the jam pan off the heat and test for set.

Test to see if it's set using the spoon, then use the following saucer test, which is slightly different to jam:

Place a tbsp of marmalade on a saucer and leave for 1 minute. If the marmalade holds together rather than drips like water all over the saucer and crinkles when you push it with your finger after 1 minute, it is set. It won't quite stay apart like jam, but it must crinkle.

If the marmalade is not set, return the pan to the heat for another couple of minutes and then test again.

When you are happy it is set, remove the jam pan from the heat and skim off any scum using a metal spoon.

Leave to cool for 10 minutes, then stir to evenly disperse the peel, ladle into jars and twist the lids on tightly.

Wipe the jars clean and, when cold (the jars, not you), label.

Taste Test: Wow! This has a powerful taste which is a bit much for me first thing in the morning, so maybe it's more of an afternoon tea time treat. The peel definitely takes a fair bit of chewing (hence the News flash), but this is Julia in the fish shop's favourite and Tai Chi Mother-in-Law's second favourite flavour. It's a good job I've got some marmalade tasters, otherwise I might be a bit disheartened.

Lemon Marmalade

I'm now a motivated marmalade maker, but motivated is not necessarily the same as good. I want the lemony hit without having to pick chewy bits of peel out of my teeth, so I'm going to make sure my peel is completely soft before adding the sugar.

My early enthusiasm is dampened when, as they say, a watched pot doesn't boil, which might be why mine took 40 minutes to reach setting point. I had to put the jars back in the oven to keep them warm, and I had only sterilised 9 and didn't have enough. I then realised why I needed more jars. The marmalade was still runny as I'd misjudged setting point AGAIN.

Why oh why won't my marmalade SET?? I thought if you could make jam you must be able to make marmalade – and I thought WRONG. Why do I have to add the pips when lemon juice is high in pectin AND I'm using the peel; Isn't this a double pectin whammy? YES. Shouldn't I only have problems setting if my marmalade is low in

pectin or acid? YES. So what is the problem?? Actually I still don't know. I think there must be a technique I'm just not getting the hang of. I need to find a little old lady to consult or get reading. No little old lady in sight, so reading it is.

No. of jars: 12 jars (if slightly under-set), so sterilise 10 medium jars. Yields about 3.3kg Time taken: 3 hours	**Ingredients** 900g / 2 lb unwaxed lemons (about 8), organic if possible 2.4 kg / 12 cups granulated sugar 2.2 litres / 9¼ cups water

How to Make

Stage One

Rinse the lemons, give them a good scrub if waxed, then halve and juice, binning the pips, and sieve the juice into the jam pan.

Cut the lemons into quarters and fold the peel back on itself to make it lie flat when you place it peel side down on the board. Then slice horizontally with a knife to remove as much of the pulpy stuff and pith as you can. The lemon peel should be dry. Take your time so that you slice finely.

Roughly chop and add the pulp to the jam pan. Check for pips, which can go in the bin. I'm actually enjoying binning them.

Slice the lemon peel finely and add it to the jam pan together with the water. If you pre-soak the sliced fruit in the water it reduces simmering time dramatically.

News flash: Definitely leave the peel to soak for at least a couple of hours.

THE JAMMY BODGER

Stage Two

Bring the jam pan to the boil, then reduce the heat, cover and simmer gently for 1½-2 hours, or until the peel is very soft. Chew it to check.

Prep the jars (cold oven 110°C / 225°F / Mk ¼ for 30 minutes) and lids, ladle and funnel (saucepan with boiling water for 20 seconds). Place 3 saucers in the fridge to test for set.

Uncover the marmalade and add the sugar, stirring constantly until completely dissolved.

Increase the heat to high and boil the marmalade rapidly. You are watching for a fast, steady boil all over the surface, and for it to thicken slightly and darken in colour.

Test to see if it's set by doing the spoon test followed by placing a tablespoon of marmalade on one of the saucers. If the marmalade holds together rather than drips like water over the saucer, and if, after 1 minute,

it crinkles when you push it with your finger, it's set. It won't quite stay apart like jam, but it must crinkle.

When you are happy with the set, remove the jam pan from the heat and skim off any scum using a metal spoon.

If the marmalade is not set, return the jam pan to the heat for another couple of minutes and then test again.

Leave to cool for 10 minutes, then stir to evenly disperse the peel, ladle into jars and twist the lids on tightly.

Taste Test: Brilliant, sharp and zesty, and not chewy at all, just err... slightly runny. Running Shop Roger commented that it could be sucked up through a straw – cheeky but true. Surprise, surprise, I still can't get setting point right, which is really frustrating. But the peel is soft, and the flavour good enough to convert professed marmalade hater Steve. Result!

Fruity Thoughts

I've read that there is as much pectin in the peel as the pips, so there is really no need to add a muslin bag of pips. To say I'm very pleased is an understatement; no more struggling with leaking pip bags for me.

It should take approximately 20 minutes of continuous boiling to hit setting point, although each marmalade varies. If it hasn't set you've got a problem, and if you carry on boiling (I know this much from experience), it ends up really dense and sticky and tastes like boiled sweets. Even if you can reset the marmalade by adding water and boiling it again, it will still be dense. My ultra-strong and stodgy textured lemon and root ginger marmalade is proof of this.

The setting point for marmalade is easy to miss, so test for set frequently. I'm watching mine like a hawk, doing a quick pip check at the same time, and it takes ages to get THERE, and then I'm not even sure it is THERE, or even where THERE is, and then it sets like a rock. I think I need to work on what THERE looks like as it doesn't seem to be the same as for jam.

If you end up with more jars than the recipe states, then the marmalade is probably under-set. If it's really runny and you can't get away with it, pour the marmalade back into the jam pan, add a good squirt of lemon juice and look for setting point again.

If you end up with the right amount of jars and it's not set, there isn't enough pectin. Maybe your fruit is a bit old and the pectin level has decreased, or check your recipe, as maybe the fruit you used wasn't high enough in pectin in the first place.

After setting point is reached and the marmalade has passed the tests for set, leave it to settle in the jam pan for 10 minutes and then stir to evenly disperse the peel. This is a cheeky way to check again if the marmalade is set as it should start to thicken slightly and form a thin, custard-like skin. If it doesn't, check with the saucer test again and think about re-boiling. It's easier to reset now than having to empty, wash and re-sterilise your jars again. I've added this into the first recipe to give you a fighting chance.

Drunken Berry Jelly

I've got frozen sloes from last year. You can play with the fruit in this recipe, but you need a tart berry like sloes, cranberries or blackcurrants, and then a gentler berry like blackberries or raspberries, or a pack of mixed summer berries. The sloes in sloe gin could also be replaced with another tart berry.

This combination helps the pectin levels, as even though the fruits are frozen, the tarter berries still only come down to medium pectin. If you've only got low pectin fruit like all frozen blackberries or blueberries, then use Jam Sugar, 1 pectin sachet or ½ a bottle of liquid pectin and lemon juice. Full instructions will be given on the bottle.

No. of jars: 4 medium jars, yielding about 1.3kg Time taken: 1½ hours not including dripping time	Ingredients
	600g / 4 cups frozen sloes (or about 550g / 3¾ cups fresh)
	400g / 3¼ cups cooking apples, chopped
	1kg / 6½ cups frozen blackberries (or 800g / 5½ cups fresh)
	1.2 litres / 5 cups cold water
	Juice of 1 Lemon (just in case)
	1kg / 5 cups granulated sugar
	45ml / 3 tbsp gin

Calculating Sugar Formula: 600ml / 2½ cups juice = 450g / 2¼ cups sugar

How to Make

Weigh and rinse the sloes and blackberries. Prick the sloes if fresh, but there is no need if your fruit is frozen. Add to the jam pan with the chopped apples (no need to peel or core), the water and the lemon juice, and bring to the boil.

Simmer for 30 minutes or until the fruit is soft and mushy. Help it out with a potato masher.

Scald your jelly bag, then ladle in the fruity mush and leave it to drip through overnight.

Prep your jars (cold oven 110°C / 225°F / Mk ¼ for 30 minutes) and lids, ladle and funnel (saucepan with boiling water for 20 seconds). Place 3 saucers in the fridge to test for set.

Pour the jelly juice into a measuring jug and work out how much sugar to add.

Pour the juice into the clean jam pan, warm the juice, then add the sugar, stirring continuously until dissolved.

Boil the jelly rapidly for about 10 minutes, and when you think it's doing the 'I'm setting' boil, start testing for set on the saucers. If it's not reaching setting point, sieve in the lemon juice.

When you're happy it's set, take the jam pan off the heat, skim off any scum, then stir in the gin.

Pour the jelly into the jars and twist the lids on tightly.

Taste Test: It's got a beautiful set. It was great. The setting point was really obvious and the flavour is tart but with depth. Fab with meat, brie or blue cheese, although Steve thinks it's great with peanut butter on toast. For some reason that makes my efforts to get a well-rounded flavour seem a little unappreciated, so I'm hiding the other jars.

Squiffy Cider Apple Jelly

I'm very excited about making this as I've got brilliant local-ish strawberry and pear cider, and I want to see if anyone can taste the flavours in the final jelly. I like cider so I was a bit gutted about the amount which went in, as when I doubled the recipe it used nearly 2 bottles and there was hardly any left for a swig!

No. of Jars: *Recipe x 2 made only 4 medium jars, yielding approximately 1.3kg. You never get as many jars out with jellies.* *Time taken: Longer than it should have as I popped back out to the shops to get the 2nd bottle of cider (and yes it was for the recipe). About 3½ hours including cooking and jelly straining*	**Ingredients** 900g / 7¼ cups cooking apples, roughly chopped 1 litre / 4¼ cups cider (fruity flavours are good) Juice and pips of 1 orange (or 2 oranges and no lemons, and vice versa) Juice and pips of 1 lemon 2 sticks cinnamon or 1 tbsp ground cinnamon (or allspice) 4 or 5 whole cloves or star anise 150ml / ⅔ cups water 1kg / 5 cups granulated sugar (max) Optional cinnamon sticks to decorate the jars or leave out the cinnamon and cloves and stir in a handful of finely chopped sage or 3-4 tsp chilli flakes after straining through the jelly bag
Calculating Sugar Formula: 600ml / 2½ cups juice = 450g / 2¼ cups sugar	

THE JAMMY BODGER

How to Make

Add your apples, cider, orange and lemon juice and pips, cinnamon stick, cloves and water to your jam pan and bring to the boil, cover and simmer for about 45 minutes.

Scald your jelly bag, then ladle the juicy pulp in and leave to drip through for a couple of hours or overnight.

Prep your jars (cold oven 110°C / 225°F / Mk ¼ for 30 minutes) and lids, ladle and funnel (saucepan with boiling water for 20 seconds). Place 3 saucers in the fridge to test for set

Pour the juice into a measuring jug and work out how much sugar to add using the Calculating Sugar Formula beneath the Ingredients.

Pour the juice into the clean jam pan and warm gently. Add the sugar, stirring continuously until dissolved, then bring the jelly to a rapid boil and boil hard until set, removing the jam pan from the heat each time you test.

When set remove the jam pan from heat and skim off any scum (there should not be much).

Leave to settle for 10 minutes, then stir to distribute evenly any added ingredients and ladle into the jars. Drop in a cinnamon stick if using.

Twist the lids on tightly and, when cold, label and

store in a dark cupboard.

Taste Test: How to describe it? It's vibrant, but not in your face like a marmalade or tart jelly. It's got real depth and keeps you coming back for more. I can't believe it but my mate Anthony Williams could name the flavours in the cider, hence I'm naming him here.

Regula Guru asks if I want some more lemons from Somerset Organic Link. I can't believe my ears when I hear myself asking if they have any oranges. I've got to stop reading jammy books late at night as it's somehow crept into my subconscious that I want to make orange marmalade. It must be curiosity as so many people, particularly the older generation, put orange marmalade on a pedestal. My new oranges are Valencias, labelled as juicers. I'm not quite sure what that means, but surely an orange is an orange? (This will come back to haunt me!)

Not Making Sweet Orange Marmalade: My first orange marmalade was such a chewy mess it wasn't worth recording. I've now got 12 jars of marmalade I can't even give away. The flavour was bland and boring, and marred by the fact that 5 minutes later you are still chewing peel.

I'm blaming my oranges for my peel teething problems. The lemon marmalade was only slightly chewy, but this marmalade is on a whole new scale of chewiness. When I looked up Valencia oranges on the Internet it said they are coarse and thick skinned, which is probably why no matter how careful I am slicing and simmering for ages, they still end up chewy. You can tell I'm not annoyed at all. I need to stop blindly following recipes and think. The lemons eventually softened, but I was simmering for ages and still struggling with the set, so I've not solved either of my marmalade issues. The problem is I don't know why it's not working. I need to try something different.

Fruity Lessons Learnt/ Things to Ponder

I refuse to think my marmalade would set if I used a bag of pips, which most recipes recommend AND I'm ignoring advice about there being no point in re-setting over-set marmalade.

I'm completely disillusioned with the saucer test for marmalade, so I'm going to use my own. If your marmalade has passed the spoon test, put a blob of marmalade on the saucer. If it's a slightly darker colour and holds together rather than all watery and translucent, and if, after a minute, it wrinkles when you push it with your finger, then your marmalade IS set. It does not need to stay completely separate like a runway through the marmalade. As this is such a crucial stage I've amended the previous recipes to take account of this as I really don't want you to repeat all my setting woes.

This is my 'Eureka' moment. The new saucer test makes all the difference. This is the first marmalade I've tried it on, and I've set it! Yes, you heard me correctly, I've set a marmalade which I am now enjoying eating.

Orange & Whisky Marmalade

If I label my marmalade thick shred at least people know what they are letting themselves in for! I'm going to try cooking the oranges whole and then juicing and slicing them. Sweet oranges obviously benefit from added flavourings, so I added brandy which I thought was the same as whisky. It turns out it's not, but it still tastes good.

When eventually I did manage to make Seville orange marmalade, it was so much easier to set, so if you're new to marmalade like me, make your life a whole lot easier and track down some Sevilles (see page 165 for Seville orange marmalade) OR why not use a mixture of oranges and lemons to up the pectin, but still get the great whisky flavour.

	Ingredients
No. of jars: 7 medium jars approximately, yielding 2.3kg, but sterilise more jars, just in case	900g / 2lb sweet oranges, unwaxed if possible (6 approx.)
Time taken: 4 hours, plus 3 hours the following day	2.4 litres / 10 cups water
	1kg / 5 cups granulated sugar
I've reduced the sugar so it will now keep for a year. If you want it to keep for up to 2 years, add 1.8kg / 9 cups	9 tbsp lemon juice (about 3 lemons)
	60ml / ¼ cup brandy or whisky

How to Make

Rinse, de-button and scrub off any dirt. Give waxed oranges a good scrub with sugar and rinse again, and then place in the jam pan with the water. You want the oranges to be covered by the water.

Simmer the oranges whole for 2-3 hours, and covered, until they can be easily pierced with a knife.

Remove the oranges, cool until they can be handled comfortably, then halve and juice them, but gently as they will be really floppy.

Cut the oranges into quarters and place them peel side down on a chopping board. Slice gently horizontally with a knife to remove as much of the pulpy stuff as possible. You want to end up with a thin piece of peel.

Roughly chop the pulp and add to the jam pan. Watch out for any hidden pips and pop them in the bin.

Slice the peel as finely as possible, unless you like it chunky. I think my fine slicing is chunky anyway.

Sieve the juice back into the jam pan together with the sliced peel.

Prep your jars (cold oven 110°C / 225°F / Mk ¼ for 30 minutes) and lids, ladle and funnel (saucepan with boiling water for 20 seconds). Place 3 saucers in the fridge to test for set.

Bring the marmalade to the boil, then reduce the heat and add the sugar, stirring constantly until it's completely dissolved.

Sieve in the lemon juice.

Heat back up, and when boiling rapidly all over the surface and the bubbles make a noise when they burst, test for set.

Test to see if it has set using the spoon test followed

THE JAMMY BODGER

by the saucer test. Place a tablespoon of marmalade on 1 of the saucers and leave for 1 minute. If the marmalade crinkles when you push it with your finger, it has set.

If the marmalade is not set, return the jam pan to the heat for another couple of minutes and test again.

When you are happy with the set, remove the jam pan from the heat and skim off any scum using a metal spoon.

Stir in the brandy or whisky.

Leave to cool for 10 minutes, then stir to evenly disperse the peel, ladle into jars and twist the lids on tightly.

Taste Test: Surprisingly people love it! Jan and Eddie from Tai Chi actually asked for another jar, so either they are being excessively polite, or maybe they are harking back to their childhood as this tastes more like a traditional marmalade. At the official marmalade taste test the testers (aka Jo and Ant) thought this had the best flavour, and that it had texture rather than chew.

What a relief. I thought I was going mad. I've just read that unlike Seville oranges, the pith of sweet oranges does not go translucent when cooked, and that sweet oranges are harder to set than bitter ones. Why couldn't I find that out earlier?? I've been trawling through jammy books and the Internet, and it's just not easy to find these things out. I need to accept that sweet oranges are always going to make a chunky orange marmalade, and need to check out what I've learnt on a Seville orange.

From chewy to crunchy: It seems if there is a mistake you can make with marmalade, I am making it. The stock pile of chewy, runny, congealed and crunchy just keeps on growing, so I need a few recipes to use them up.

Orange & Walnut Flapjacks

This is the first time I understood what was meant by a tray bake, so thanks to The Lady of the Lakes (aka Steve's mum, but that name sounded so much more exciting).

Ingredients

225g / 1 cup (2 sticks) butter, diced

170g / ⅞ cup caster sugar

3 tbsp golden syrup / honey / maple syrup

270g / 3 cups porridge oats

50g / ⅓ cup walnut bits

Zest of 1 orange, or finely chopped candied peel

5 tbsp marmalade

How to Make

Preheat the oven to 190°C / 375°F / Mk 5 and grease a shallow baking tray.

Melt the butter, sugar and syrup in a large saucepan over a medium heat.

Remove from the heat and stir in the oats, walnuts and peel or zest.

Pour into the baking tray and cook for 30 minutes until the edges are golden, but it's still springy in the middle.

Warm the marmalade in a small saucepan and mix with a tiny bit of water to make a thick sauce, then spread over the flapjack.

Leave to cool for a couple of minutes, then mark out the bars. Leave to cool completely before cutting out or eat some whilst still warm.

FEBRUARY

Pineapple & Passionfruit Jelly

There are no fresh pineapples available, but as I'm on a mission I get 4 tins of pineapple chunks in juice, along with some emergencies-only lemons. This should be interesting. I'm not sure what I think about using tinned tropical fruit; it's been shipped rather than flown, so in theory it could be more eco, but what about the fruity benefits, the vitamin C levels and all that. They must have deteriorated, and surely there's no pectin in a tin of fruit? I can't answer that, but luckily M. Patten comes to the rescue for converting normal recipes to using tinned fruit. She states:

"If canned in syrup, you need to reduce the amount of sugar used with the fruit. (If heavy syrup reduce by about ½). If canned in natural juice, you should use the normal amount of sugar. In either case increase the amount of lemon juice in the recipe. Where no lemon juice is used in the recipe with fresh fruit add 1 tablespoon to each 450g / 1lb (2¼ cups) sugar. (And where lemon juice is used add 1 tablespoon more.)"
The Jams, Preserves and Chutneys Handbook; 1995.

Once again I had the right number of jars, but was left with a jellified syrup. There's absolutely NO pectin in this jelly, and the lemon juice didn't help at all. Firmer action is required. I'm calling in the big guns.

I'm going to use jam sugar. You could use a pectin sachet, liquid pectin (but with no need to add lemon juice as the pineapple is already highly acidic), or add 2 chopped up lemons to the fruit pulp before it drips through the jelly bag, although this will alter the flavour. Jam sugar worked perfectly, and wow, it set really quickly.

No. of jars: 5 small jars *Time taken: 30 minutes prep, 1½ hours simmering, 3 hours or overnight dripping through the jelly bag and 1 hour to sort and set the next day*	**Ingredients** 2 medium pineapples, peeled and coarsely chopped Or 4 tins of pineapple, (about 900g / 5 cups) 4 passionfruit, halved, with seeds and pulp scooped out 900ml / 3¾ cups water 1kg / 5 cups jam sugar (at most) OR granulated sugar (white) + 1 sachet pectin, or pectin stock, or ½ bottle liquid pectin
Calculating Sugar Formula: 600ml / 2½ cups juice = 450g / 2¼ cups sugar	

How to Make

Add the passionfruit juice and the fresh chopped pineapple to the jam pan with the water (and juice from the tins, if using) and bring to the boil. Cover and simmer for 1½-2 hours until the fruit is soft.

Use a hand blender or pour the fruity pulp into a food processor and blend until nearly puréed.

Scald the jelly bag, then ladle the fruity pulp into the jelly bag and leave it to drip through.

THE JAMMY BODGER

Prep the jars (cold oven 110°C / 225°F / Mk ¼ for 30 minutes) and lids, ladle and funnel (saucepan with boiling water for 20 seconds). Place 3 saucers in the fridge to test for set.

Pour the jelly juice into a measuring jug and calculate the amount of sugar to be added.

Warm the juice in the clean jam pan and, when warm, add the sugar. If using pectin sachets add now. Stir continuously until dissolved.

Increase the heat, stop stirring and boil hard for 5–10 minutes, or until the jelly reaches setting point.

Remove the jam pan from the heat to test for set and when you are happy with the set, take the pan off the heat. Stir gently in one direction to disperse the foam, then skim off the scum.

Ladle or pour the jelly into the jars, twist the lids on tightly, then leave on a cake rack to cool.

Taste Test: I tasted this a few times as I went along and it's really fruity without being sickly sweet or overly tart. You might eat it as a pudding on its own or mix it with a warm sponge in a sticky pudding. I think I might just eat some now.

Fruity Lessons Learnt / Things to Ponder

Know your fruit, and if possible your fruit seller too. If I could guarantee my fruit is fresh and hadn't been sitting on the supermarket shelf wilting for weeks (I don't even know what a wilted pineapple looks like), I doubt if I would have had the same pectin problems.

If you're using low pectin fruits, keep some pectin in your cupboard for emergencies. I think jam sugar is the easiest option when you are starting out, but if you are struggling for set and need to add something, think lemons first, then sachets or liquid pectin.

Lemon Syrupy Stodge Cake

I make different versions of this cake all the time using up any leftovers of recipes or unset jelly, which I've used here in place of the milk and then mixed some more with the icing sugar. Read over the recipe before starting to decide which version of the ingredients you are using.

How to Make

Grease an 800g loaf tin or small round tin.

Cream together **175g / ⅞ cup sugar, 115g / ½ cup (1 stick) butter, 175g / 1½ cups self raising flour** and **2 eggs**.

Add the zest of **2 lemons** OR **candied peel** OR if using unset jelly syrup don't add anything unless you've got lemon leftovers.

Add **2 tbsp milk** OR **jelly syrup** until you have dropping consistency.

Pour into the cake tin and bake at 180°C / 350°F / Mk 4 for 45-50 minutes or until when you insert a sharp knife it comes out clean.

Sieve about **125g / 1 cup icing sugar** into a small bowl and add **lemon juice** OR **jelly syrup** gradually until it forms a runny enough paste to pour.

Prick the cake all over with a knife or skewer and

slowly pour over the Icing. If you wait until a bit is absorbed before pouring more you will lose less through it draining off down the side of the tin. Or break up the cake, pop it into a cake tin with a lid, pour over the icing and take it around to a friend's house to share.

Scatter candied peel over the top, if using.

Leave the cake in the tin until cold, or if you can't wait, turn it out when slightly warm and enjoy.

Orange, Grapefruit & Lemon Marmalade

I simmered the fruit for 3 hours until the oranges and lemons nearly collapsed when pierced. I wanted the peel really soft. But it just wasn't boiling right. It boiled in a central funnel, not all over the surface. As I am beginning not to trust my judgement on setting (I can't think why), I unwrapped my Christmas present jam thermometer, warmed it in the sterilising saucepan, and plunged it into the jam pan.

The temperature as per usual hovers persistently just below the setting temperature of 105°C / 222°F; this I can only tell after quickly removing the thermometer and wiping away the steam. If you aren't quick enough the temperature drops, so you are none the wiser. I whipped the jam pan off the heat when the marmalade was at last at the correct temperature, but it wasn't set and needed another couple of minutes back on the heat. Reaching the right temperature is the same as seeing the 'I'm setting' boil, and means it's starting to set, not that it's set. The saucer test is the real test, which is why I don't think a jam thermometer is particularly useful.

I eventually ended up with a fab tasting marmalade, so struggles for setting aside, this is definitely worth making.

| No. of jars: 7 medium jars, approximately, yielding 2.2kg

Time taken: About 3 hours and 45 minutes | **Ingredients**

1kg / 2lb 4oz oranges (5), grapefruit (1), lemons (2) approximately

2kg / 10 cups granulated sugar

2.5 litres / 10½ cups water |
| --- | --- |

How to Make

Rinse and gently scrub and de-button the fruit and place it whole in the jam pan with the water.

Bring the fruit to the boil, then reduce the heat for the long simmer. Simmer covered for 2 to 3 hours until the fruit is really soft and can be pierced easily. The grapefruit will look like it's got a puncture.

Remove the fruit from the water (keeping the water in the pan), and when the fruit is cool, gently juice it, flicking the pips into a bowl to bin later. Sieve the juice into the jam pan.

Slice the peel as finely as possible, keeping an eye out for any stray pips, and put it back into the jam pan. Chop up the fruity pulp left from the oranges and add that to the jam pan too, but get rid of any stringy bits.

Warm the fruity pulp, add the sugar and stir over a low heat until completely dissolved.

Prep the jars (cold oven 110°C / 225°F / Mk ¼ for 30 minutes) and lids, ladle and funnel (saucepan with boiling water for 20 seconds). Place 3 saucers in the fridge to test for set.

Bring the marmalade to a rapid boil, and when you think it's ready do the spoon test followed by the saucer test: a tablespoon of marmalade on 1 of the saucers, and left for 1 minute. If the marmalade crinkles when pushed with your finger, it's set.

If the marmalade is not set, return the jam pan to the heat for another couple of minutes and then test again.

When you are happy with the set, remove the jam pan from the heat and skim off any scum using a metal spoon.

Leave to cool for 10 minutes, then stir to evenly disperse the peel, ladle into jars and twist the lids on tightly.

Taste Test: Yippee! It doesn't look quite the same in print, but it's about the noise I made. At last! There's a good flavour from the grapefruit which lifts the sweetness of the orange and, wonders will never cease, it's not too chewy!

Finally Seville oranges: I'm so excited and I just can't hide it. The butcher came up trumps with Seville oranges, and although they wouldn't win a beauty contest (the oranges, that is), I can't wait to see what the flavour is like. I can't stop myself from buying more and more. I've rinsed and weighed the extras into 4 large sandwich bags - 1kg of oranges in each, and although I don't know how to make marmalade from frozen oranges, I'm too jubilant to care.

Seville oranges aren't pleasant to eat, and not only because of the taste, but also because they are pithy and pippy, but I just can't wait to try the marmalade. I feel fully prepared for this momentous occasion because I must have learnt a few basic things from making marmalade.

Seville Orange Marmalade

No. of jars: 6½ medium jars, yielding about 2.1kg	Ingredients
Time taken: 1 hour then overnight, then 2 hours simmering, then 40 minutes nearly setting, then set – 3hrs 40mins in total	1.1kg / 2lb 6oz Seville oranges (about 8)
	1.2 kg / 6 cups granulated sugar
	1.9 litres / 8 cups water

How to Make

Day 1

Rinse and de-button the oranges and give them a gentle scrub on any discoloured sections.

Halve and juice them, binning the pips, and sieve the juice into the jam pan.

Cut the halves into quarters and fold the peel back on itself to make it lie flat when you place it peel side down on the board. Slice horizontally with a knife to remove as much of the pulpy stuff and pith as you can. The orange peel should be dry.

Roughly chop and add the pulp to the jam pan, but check for pips. There are a lot of them, which can go in the bin.

Slice the orange peel finely, remembering you've got all the time in the world.

Add the orange peel and water to the jam pan and leave to soak overnight.

Day 2

Bring the orange peely juice to the boil, reduce the heat, cover with the lid (but leaving some space for air to escape) and simmer gently for 1½-2 hours, or

THE JAMMY BODGER

JAMMY TIP

Seville oranges are unlikely to be waxed as they are purely for marmalade makers. No-one would be mad enough to eat one raw. This means no manic scrubbing is required.

until the peel is very soft. Chew it to check.

Prep the jars (cold oven 110°C / 225°F / Mk ¼ for 30 minutes) and lids, ladle and funnel (saucepan with boiling water for 20 seconds). Place 3 saucers in the fridge to test for set.

Uncover the marmalade and add the sugar, stirring constantly until completely dissolved.

Heat the marmalade without stirring until it's boiling rapidly, then, when you think it's set, start testing.

Scoop some marmalade up and out, allow it to cool for about 20 seconds, then turn the spoon on its side above the jam pan. If it runs together and drips off in a jellified lump or two, then take the jam pan off the heat and place a tablespoon of marmalade on one of the saucers. Leave it for 1 minute and if the marmalade crinkles when you push it with your finger, it's set.

If the marmalade is not set, return the jam pan to the heat for another couple of minutes and then test again.

When you are happy with the set remove the jam pan

from the heat and skim off any scum using a metal spoon.

Leave to cool for 10 minutes, then stir to evenly disperse the peel, ladle into jars and twist the lids on tightly.

Wipe the jars clean and label when cool.

Taste Test: I'm so impressed. The flavour has so much more depth than any of the other marmalades and even the orange and lemon marmalade can't match this bitter sweetness. Seville orange marmalade on toast v. Marmite on toast? The marmalade wins hands down. It's a real revelation and I can see why some people just don't bother making marmalade with anything else, but I think they'd be pleasantly surprised that some of the others do have something to offer.

I've tried marmalade made from tins (I think they are called MaMade, thank you Steve at the pharmacy), but the flavour just doesn't compare. Also, I can't believe I'm saying this, but I missed the peel as the tinned version is more like a jelly marmalade with only fine slivers added back in. This is such a success I can't believe it.

Fruity Lessons Learnt / Things to Ponder

Wow! (This word has been used a lot in this section.)

It seems the whole fruit method itself leads to a chunkier marmalade, no matter what oranges you use, so it's not that I'm rubbish at this (although I admit I did wonder it at one point).

But also if you presoak your sliced fruit overnight and then make marmalade the next day, you've already started softening the peel, and this reduces the cooking time. Sounds good to me.

The main lesson I learnt from all my other marmalades is... wait for it... making marmalade is not the same as making jam.

It takes a lot more time to make marmalade, because each stage cannot be rushed, and even setting point will only come when the marmalade is ready. It will not be dictated to by heat or thermometer. Marmalade won't boil as madly and with such wild abandon as jam, and you've just got to keep checking for set as it won't look much different to a full on boil. Marmalade is like a little old lady taking her time to cross the road. She will not be hurried, and it's best not to try and rush her.

MARCH

It's still not much fun on the home-grown fruity front, and I don't fancy forced rhubarb. What's it being forced to do? Grow a month earlier in warm sheds where it grows by candlelight and you can hear it growing in the night. What's the rush when I can have naturally grown rhubarb in May, and the free and happy rhubarb is already on its way. But this does make March and April the lean, mean, quiet months. It's going to be May before everything is hip and happening. So let's make the most of the citrus season.

I am making two preserves in one day as my massive batch of lemons are starting to go soggy. I've bought oranges from Cyprus, well I bought them from the local supermarket as that would have been too far to go, and the packaging says they've been chosen for their unique flavour, so fingers crossed.

I was admiring this jelly's 'I'm setting' boil as you could really hear the bubbles burst. I took the jam pan off the heat and tested, not yet, and then, a minute later I turned the spoon on its side and it dripped off completely jellified. I whacked the jam pan off the heat, but it was too late. The jelly had over-set. I'm not joking; this set quickly. It wasn't ruined, but it was firmer than I'd like, and I had to warm the jam pan up to pot it as after I'd skimmed the scum it started to set in the pan.

The Bells of St Clements Jelly

No. of jars: 2nd time round I got 3 large jars, yielding about 1.4kg. As usual with jelly it's better off in small jars, so sterilise 8	Ingredients
	1kg / 2lb 4oz lemons unwaxed and organic if possible (about 7)
	500g / 1lb 2oz sweet oranges, unwaxed if possible (about 3)
Time taken: It felt like days because I made lemon and root ginger marmalade at the same time, but realistically about 4½ hours of activity	1kg / 5 cups granulated sugar
	2.8 litres / 11¾ cups water
Calculating Sugar Formula: 600ml / 2½ cups juice = 450g / 2¼ cups sugar	

How to Make

Day 1 – scrub and stew

Rinse the fruit and give it a scrub with a brush or rough cloth and sugar if it is waxed. Remove the peel as thinly as possible with a potato peeler or sharp knife, then slice finely and tie the peel up tightly in a muslin square with kitchen string.

Roughly chop up the fruit and place it (pips and all) into the jam pan with the muslin bag.

Add the water, then cover the jam pan (I find my wok lid fits) and leave to stew overnight.

Day 2 – let's make jelly

Simmer the fruit for 1½-2 hours until it's really mushy.

Scald your jelly bag and set up the stand and bowl.

JAMMY TIP

The easiest way to remove peel is to top and tail the fruit, thus removing the dodgy bits of peel at both ends. Then use a peeler to pare off thin slices of peel into a bowl, leaving the fruit covered in a thick layer of pith. Put the (thinly sliced for marmalade) peel into the muslin bag.

THE JAMMY BODGER

When the fruit is mushy, take out the muslin bag and put it in a bowl. Do not discard it. Open the bag and check if the peel is soft, and if not pop it back in the jam pan and simmer everything for another 20 minutes, then check again.

Ladle the fruity pulp into the jelly bag and leave to drain until all the juice is through – do not prod or poke. This takes at least a couple of hours, or leave it overnight.

Day 3 – set

Prep the jars (cold oven then 110°C / 225°F / Mk ¼ for 30 minutes) and lids, ladle and funnel (saucepan with boiling water for 20 seconds). Place 3 saucers in the fridge to test for set.

Measure the juice in a measuring jug, then pour into the clean jam pan. Using the Calculating Sugar Formula beneath the Ingredients, work out how much sugar to add.

Heat the juice until warm, then add the sugar, stirring continuously until completely dissolved.

Pop the muslin bag into the jam pan (or if making jelly marmalade, empty its contents into the jam pan, being careful there are no hidden pips), and increase the heat until it boils rapidly.

Boil hard for 5-10 minutes, but keep a close eye on it and check for setting point every couple of minutes, taking the jam pan off the heat each time.

When you are happy with the set, squeeze the muslin bag with the tongs and remove (unless you've already emptied it) and skim off any scum.

Allow to cool for 10 minutes, then stir to evenly distribute the peel, ladle into the jars and twist the lids on tightly.

Taste Test: It's sweet and bitter, probably due to the

thick layer of pith that's left on the fruit. I think I like it. I will have to wait for breakfast to be sure. Regula Guru suggests a tbsp could be added to a Moroccan lamb tagine in place of preserved lemons or lemon zest. I just had it on toast for breakfast and it's a winner – yeah!

Lemon Posset

Put roughly **600ml / 2½ cups double cream** (heavy cream) in a saucepan with **100g / ½ cup caster sugar** and bring to the boil, then simmer for 2 or 3 minutes. Remove from the heat and whisk in **the juice and zest of 2 lemons**. Place a dollop of **lemon curd (optional)** in the bottom of 4 glasses or dishes, then pour on the posset. Leave to chill for 3-4 hours in the fridge, or even better overnight. I ate mine for breakfast. Classy!

Compost Fruit Jelly

The idea is to use up leftover apple cores and peelings, and orange peelings from other recipes, and came from Pam Corbin, author of 'Preserves.' You can use any type of oranges with this recipe as it doesn't rely purely on the oranges for flavour. I added grapefruit juice simply because I had a carton of it in the fridge and thought it would add some acidity to the recipe. I ended up with 1 litre of juice plus the glass of grapefruit juice, so I used 750g sugar. When looking to set the jelly the jam pan didn't seem to get hot enough, and it only did a whole pan boil once, so I was a bit worried about the set, but it was fine.

This jelly changes to a slightly darker colour once it has reached setting point, but you can't really see it through all the bubbles and scum until you've taken it off the heat. If it doesn't look any darker, make sure it stays separate on the saucer as with any jelly.

No. of jars: 2 small jars, yielding about 960g Time taken: 2 hours first thing, and just over an hour after it dripped through the jelly bag	Ingredients
	500g / 1lb 2oz apple cores and peel
	500g / 1lb 2oz citrus peel (unwaxed lemon, orange, grapefruit, lime) cut into roughly 1cm / ⅓ inch shreds
	1kg / 5 cups granulated sugar (you won't need all of this)
	1.5 litres / 6⅓ cups water
	Juice of 1 orange, lemon or grapefruit (optional)

Calculating Sugar Formula: 600ml / 2½ cups juice = 450g / 2¼ cups sugar

How to Make

Add the apple cores, peel and the citrus peel to your jam pan and add enough water to cover. Simmer for 45-60 minutes to soften the fruit and help release the pectin.

Scald your jelly bag and set up the stand.

When the fruit has softened, ladle it into the jelly bag and leave to drip through.

Prep the jars (cold oven then 110°C / 225°F / Mk ¼ for 30 minutes) and lids, ladle and funnel (saucepan with boiling water for 20 seconds). Place 3 saucers in the fridge to test for set.

Remove the jelly bag and tip the juice from the bowl into a measuring jug, note the amount, then pour the juice into the jam pan.

Work out how much sugar you need to add.

Heat the juice and when warm add the sugar and stir until fully dissolved.

Boil rapidly without stirring until you are happy it has set, then remove from the heat. Skim off any scum, pot and twist the lids on tightly.

Wipe down the jars and celebrate.

Taste Test: It's got a great silky texture and Julia in the fish shop has used it as a kind of chutney, something which I hadn't thought of.

Lemon & Lime Marmalade

This needs to soak beforehand. The jammy books warn that lemon peel can be tough and hard to slice, but that's nothing compared to lime. I'm adding the lemon and lime juice later in the recipe to see if this helps it set, as maybe if they are added at the start the pectin may get boiled or killed off like Vitamin C.

No. of jars: 11 small and medium jars, yielding about 3.2kg	Ingredients
Time taken: About 2hrs 45 minutes (not including soaking time)	1.3kg / 2 lb 14oz fruit (or about 6 lemons and limes)
	2.6kg / 13 cups granulated sugar
	2.8 litres / 11¾ cups water

How to Make

Rinse the fruit and if waxed give it a good scrub with some sugar, then rinse.

Juice the fruit and keep the juice to one side to use later.

Finely slice the peel, binning the pips, and if there's loads of pith, remove some of it so the marmalade isn't too bitter.

Put the peel and the water (but not the juice yet) into the jam pan, cover and leave to soak for a couple of hours.

Simmer the peely water for 2 hours or until the peel is tender. Taste it to check.

Prep the jars (cold oven 110°C / 225°F / Mk ¼ for 30 minutes) and lids, ladle and funnel (saucepan with boiling water for 20 seconds). Place 3 saucers in the fridge to test for set.

Reduce the heat and add the sugar, stirring continuously until completely dissolved.

Sieve in the juice you set aside earlier.

Heat the marmalade without stirring until it boils rapidly. Test for set by lifting your wooden spoon out of the jam pan, holding it for 20 seconds, then turning it on one side. Your are looking for jellified drips. Take the jam pan off the heat and do the saucer test, and if it wrinkles after 1 minute on the saucer, it's set.

When you are happy with the set, remove the jam pan from the heat and skim off the scum.

Leave to stand for 10 minutes until it thickens slightly. If it doesn't thicken, return to the heat and test for set again.

Stir to evenly disperse the peel and ladle through a funnel into jars, twisting the lids on tightly.

Taste Test: Lemony and limey heaven. I've given the last of my luscious lemons a good send off.

Fruity Things to Ponder

Pectin matters! By the time I used some of my fruit it had been sitting in the cool box for a while. I thought as long as it looked fresh and fruity it would be fine, but it wasn't.

APRIL & MAY

By April the winter solstice is over and home grown fruity wonders are stirring once more, but to be honest not much is happening YET. This is the time of rest for jam makers everywhere as it's the nearly month. All early summer fruits are nearly ready, but not quite, and the zesty fruits have nearly passed their prime, but not quite.

Steve and I attempted to identify the different bushes, trees and shrubs on the hills and in the lanes around us. We were looking for hawthorn, blackthorn, blackberry, rowan and rosehip. So we wandered around with a little tree book and after an hour we weren't much the wiser. All the bushes were really straggly and windswept, but at least the blackthorn are just starting to flower, so we could spot them. It's much easier to identify bushes when they are in flower, as otherwise you are just looking at a mish mash of twigs.

Tree	Flowers	Fruit
Apple	May/June	Sept-Dec
Elder	June/July	Sept-Oct
Rose	June/July	Sept-Nov
Hawthorn	May	Aug-Oct
Plum	April	Aug-Oct
Bramble	May	Aug-Oct
Rowan	May	Aug-Sept
Crab apple	May	Oct-Nov
Blackthorn	April	Oct-Nov

You can note where the bushes are in your diary or calendar and then go and scavenge their berries later in the year. Also, once you've identified them in flower then you start to recognise them when they are not. This momentous decision meant we could go home and stop getting damp feet.

What we did find were nettle flowers, which didn't taste of much. We also picked new nettle shoots less than about 20cm high, including stems, leaves and flowers. If you pick from the underside of the leaves they don't sting, or if like us you don't really believe this, wear gloves. Pick from somewhere safe from doggy wee, then simply rinse and stew the nettle leaves in boiling water to make nettle tea. The tea is surprisingly nice and much better than bought nettle tea which can be bitter. You can also make nettle soup and probably use them for everything you would wild garlic.

We also picked loads of wild garlic. It's great raw or slightly wilted with brie, or added to lasagne, or you can pesto the lot with just olive oil and a bit of salt and lemon juice. Whatever you do, do it quickly after picking as the garlic wilts fast.

But I'm not quite happy to hang up my jam apron yet as my freezer is still full of frozen fruit. That's not a massive boast as it's a small freezer. I've got sliced apples, a batch of sliced plums labelled for plum crumble cake and another 400g batch unlabelled, so freestyle, plus plums in syrup. I've also got bought frozen fruit; 2 x 500g bags of blackberries, 340g of mixed berries, 3 x 340g of raspberries and a few cranberries.

I've made jam successfully with frozen fruit and jelly, err... well not quite as successfully, but I was using fruit I froze myself, and high pectin fruit at that. The bought frozen fruit should be nearly as good, and us customers are always assured they are picked and frozen on the same day, or am I confusing them with frozen peas. But I'm not going to take any chances. This is the month of rest and all that, so I'm going to add pectin to make sure it sets. I've got jam sugar and liquid pectin which I bought in the summer, but large supermarkets should still stock it now.

Berry Bonanza Jam

No. of jars: 6 medium jars, yielding about 1.9kg	Ingredients
	340g / 1⅓ cups frozen raspberries (340g pack)
Time taken: so quick the jam had to wait for me to sterilise the lids. About 20 minutes	450g / 3 cups frozen blackberries (500g pack)
	210g / 2 cups frozen cranberries
	900g / 4½ cups granulated sugar
	200ml / ¾ cup water
	Juice of 2 lemons (only needed if using liquid pectin, otherwise optional)
	1 bottle liquid pectin (shaken) OR 2 pectin sachets with a 3rd on standby OR jam sugar instead of granulated sugar

Don't be fooled by the weight on a frozen berry packet. Sometimes they include the weight of the container, or the fruit goes on a diet, as the frozen fruit itself sometimes weighs 50g less than stated.

JAMMY TIP

As the fruit is frozen I treated the 1kg of fruit like 900g and added 900g of sugar with the juice of ½ a lemon, boiled it, then added ¾ of a bottle of liquid pectin. It should be ½ a bottle for low pectin fruit, so

I increased it to ¾ of a bottle to be sure. I tasted the pectin – it's foul like old lemons with a hint of dead apples, but if it does the job I just don't care.

It's weird. You can't really test for set with liquid pectin. The good bit is that the fruit doesn't need to boil manically while looking for a set, which is good with frozen fruit which is already collapsing. I simply stirred it in then watched. It seemed to form a skin on the top, but didn't thicken the jam which wasn't dripping in jellified lumps off the spoon. Still the bottle doesn't mention testing for set, just stirring and potting, so I will have to wait and see. Well I waited, and I've now changed the recipe to 1 bottle and the juice of 2 lemons, as I'm just not sure of the set. It's better than some of my slippery jams, but I've added pectin, so I want a good set.

How to Make

Weigh the fruit and add to the jam pan. Rinse and weigh the cranberries last. Thankfully it all added up to an easy amount to deal with.

Add the water and simmer gently to try and release any remnants of pectin.

Prep the jars (cold oven 110°C / 225°F / Mk ¼ for 30 minutes) and lids, ladle and funnel (saucepan with boiling water for 20 seconds). Place 3 saucers in the fridge to test for set.

When the berries are soft, add the sugar and stir until dissolved, then add the lemon juice.

Boil hard for 2-3 minutes, then remove from the heat. Stir in the liquid pectin, if using.

If you are using jam sugar or pectin sachets, continue to boil rapidly until set, and test using the saucer method as normal.

Taste Test: Wow, it's so fruity it nearly made me wince. I think next time I'd sieve out the raspberry pips and make a jelly, but as usual it's only me who is bothered by them.

Plum Jam (frozen)

I'm not going to freeze sliced plums again. They look brown and dejected, and when you start to warm them they don't smell fruity and fresh like other frozen fruit. They smell like a knackered version of the plums they once were, with no fruity vibrancy left. But their flavour is still good and the jam set great if slightly darker than normal.

	Ingredients
No. of jars 6 medium jars, yielding about 1.9kg	1.1kg / 2lb 7oz de-stoned frozen plums
Time taken: 30 minutes (this adding pectin lark sure speeds up jam making)	1kg / 5 cups jam sugar
	Juice of 1 lemon

How to Make

Prep the jars (cold oven 110°C / 225°F / Mk ¼ for 30 minutes) and lids, ladle and funnel (saucepan with boiling water for 20 seconds). Place 3 saucers in the fridge to test for set.

Tip your plums into the jam pan, add the lemon juice and warm over a low heat. You shouldn't need to add water, but if plums are sticking to the jam pan, add a teeny amount.

When the plums are no longer frozen, stir in the jam sugar and stir continuously until dissolved.

Increase the heat and as soon as it's boiling all over the surface, start testing for set. Take the jam pan off the heat each time as it will set fast.

When you are happy with the set, stir gently in one direction to disperse any foam.

Skim off the scum. This will take a while. If the jam sets, just warm it gently.

Ladle into jars and twist the lids on tightly.

Taste test: I'm still loving plum jam, but it does lack a little vibrancy when compared with the fresh fruit version. But if you didn't taste them both together you'd never know, and would just think this a fab jam.

I want to use frozen berries without worrying about their pectin, so what about curds? Can you make a curd with frozen fruit? I need to stop dithering and just try it out. I used my lemon curd recipe as a base, but used raspberries. I sieved them, not because of my pips phobia, but because you really need a smooth texture in a curd as creamy butteriness and crunch don't work together.

After several goes and trips to the shop for more berries (well so much for emptying the freezer!), I can get the flavour I like, but not quite the thickness, as when I add more egg yolks to thicken the curd, the creaminess overwhelms the tart, fruity flavour. I tried adding cornflour and water paste, which did thicken the curd, but made it taste like wallpaper paste, or at least what I imagine wallpaper paste tastes like. Cooking the curd directly in the saucepan rather than bain marie style also works, but you do end up with a stickier, thicker texture. I'm going to stick with the bain marie method and if the curd is a little thin I'll just keep it in the fridge as the cold thickens it.

Raspberry Curd

I'm really enjoying using frozen berries. As there is no fruit prep everything is quick and easy.

No. of jars: 2 medium jars yielding about 650g	Ingredients
	500g / 2 cups frozen raspberries
Time taken: 40 minutes, and that's why it's best to get your jars and lids sorted first	3 medium eggs
	250g / 1¼ cups caster sugar (increase the sugar to 300g if you wish to keep the curd for longer)
	60g/¼ cup (½ stick) butter

How to Make

Prep the jars (cold oven 110°C / 225°F / Mk ¼ for 30 minutes) and lids, ladle and funnel (saucepan with boiling water for 20 seconds).

Warm the raspberries gently in a saucepan with a little water until mushy.

Push through a sieve into a large, heatproof bowl.

Add the butter and sugar to the bowl and balance the bowl over a saucepan of fast simmering water, bain marie style. The base of the bowl must not touch the water.

Stir until the butter and sugar have dissolved, then take off the heat and sieve in the egg, stirring continuously until it is all mixed in.

Continue to warm over a medium heat, stirring continuously as the curd starts to thicken. When the curd is thick and glossy and coats the back of a

THE JAMMY BODGER

wooden spoon it is ready.

Ladle into the jars, twist on the lids and leave to cool.

Place in the fridge to thicken or keep in a cool dark cupboard for 2 months tops.

Taste Test: Tart and heavenly. I swirled this into vanilla ice cream, popped it back in the freezer, and hey presto, raspberry ripple.

Monika's Dandelion Jelly

When Monika mentioned this recipe I thought she was joking. But picking dandelions is a perfect excuse to do very little but claim you are weeding on a lovely sunny day. Watch out for bees and check the dandelion heads for insects before bagging them. Also keep off areas surrounded by doggy poo bins, as where there's poo there's wee. This is fun to make as it's amazing to get a preserve from a weed that's everywhere.

	Ingredients
No. of jars: 4 small jars, but I think it should make 8 small jars, yielding about 1.4kg	500 dandelion heads approx.
	750ml / 3⅛ cups boiling water
Time taken: 30 minutes to pick, 30 minutes - 1 hour to de-flower, 15 minutes in the jam pan, left overnight, then 45 minutes to sort out	1kg / 5 cups jam sugar OR granulated sugar with ½ bottle liquid pectin OR granulated sugar with 1 pectin sachet
	Juice of 1 lemon

How to Make

Stage 1 – pick and stew

Pick the dandelion heads when they are in full flower. I counted 100 into four different bags so that even if I lost count I could compare it to the other bags.

Back home twist the green section of each dandelion head to release the petals into the jam pan. This does takes a while.

Cover the petals with the boiling water, bring back to the boil, cool and then pour into a large bowl. Cover and leave overnight in the fridge or in a cold room to infuse. (I left mine in the jam pan with a lid on, but I have 2 jam pans, so this worked OK.)

Stage 2- make jelly

Prep the jars (cold oven 110°C / 225°F / Mk ¼ for 30 minutes) and lids, ladle and funnel (saucepan with boiling water for 20 seconds). Place 3 saucers in the fridge to test for set.

Sieve the dandelion juice into a jam pan and heat to boiling point. Add the sugar and lemon juice (and pectin sachets if using).

Stir until the sugar is completely dissolved and bring back to a rapid boil for 1 minute. Take off the heat and add liquid pectin now, if using.

Test for set, then keep testing every minute until it has set.

Skim off any scum and pour into jars, twisting the lids on tightly.

When the jars are cold label them 'Confiture de Petales de Pissenlit,' which is French for dandelion, and literally means 'bed wetter'! But honestly, this is the preserve's name.

Taste Test: Once again I'm let down by not identifying the setting point correctly. I over-set this, but what a result. It's like a sticky honey with a sweet tang, and a slightly bitter aftertaste. I'm definitely going to make it again. On a taste test with a 3 year old she knew which sugary one she preferred compared to other jellies, and it was clearly this one.

Apricot & Almond Conserve

You get a lot of conserve here for a little effort as the fruit doesn't need to be picked or prepped. You'd imagine this amount of sugar would create an overly sweet, sickly jam, but once the apricots puff up you've got a lot of fruit to sweeten.

Most dried apricots nowadays are ready to eat, so don't need much presoaking, but the longer you pre-soak, the shorter the cooking time. I soaked mine for about 2 hours, simply because that was how long I was at the shops for, buying the almonds and chatting. You could leave the apricots whole after soaking, but I wasn't sure whether I might end up

THE JAMMY BODGER

with large lumps of fruit in a watery preserve, so I quartered them. I think appearance-wise whole looks better, eating-wise quartered.

No. of jars: 7 medium jars, yielding about 1.5-2kg	Ingredients
	450g / 1lb / 3½ cups dried apricots
Time taken: 1½ hours not including time soaking the apricots	1.35kg / 6¾ cups granulated sugar
	50-75g / ½-¾ cup sliced, ready to use almonds
	4 tbsp lemon juice
	2 medium lemons

How to Make

Soak the apricots in approximately 1 litre / 4¼ cups of water for at least an hour.

Prep the jars (cold oven 110°C / 225°F / Mk ¼ for 30 minutes) and lids, ladle and funnel (saucepan with boiling water for 20 seconds). Place 3 saucers in the fridge to test for set.

Put the apricots and the liquid in which they have been soaking into the jam pan. If you wish use scissors to quarter the apricots.

Bring the apricots to the boil, then cover and simmer gently for 30 minutes, or until they are completely soft.

Stir in the sugar and keep stirring until completely dissolved.

Sieve in the lemon juice and add the almonds.

Increase the heat and look to set the conserve. It should only take about 10 minutes.

When it's set, take the jam pan off the heat, stir in one direction to get rid of the foam, skim off any scum and then leave the conserve to settle in the jam pan for 10 minutes.

When the conserve has thickened slightly, stir to evenly distribute the fruit and almonds, then pot, twisting the lids on tightly.

If the almonds are hanging at the top of the jars don't worry. Leave them for a few minutes and then every time you walk past the jars give them a quick shake to redistribute the almonds. When the conserve has thickened it will hold them suspended in it.

Taste Test: It looks great with the almonds suspended in it and tastes really vibrant. I think the flavour is much stronger from the dried fruit.

Lime Tree Jelly

After watching me pick the dandelion heads Regula obviously realised I'd try anything (once), and gave me a German recipe to make lime tree jelly. It's a posh jelly as its ingredients include Champagne and a vanilla pod. These ingredients alone would give any jelly a good flavour.

After forgetting about it for a few weeks (well OK, a month), it was the start of June before I went to pick the leaves and flowers from the lime / linden trees in the park and by the side of the football pitch. All the trees' leaves were covered in sticky black stuff, but there was no sign of any aphids, so I convinced myself that maybe this was the syrupy stuff I wanted. I picked the leaves and flowers anyway as I'd bought the other ingredients, but by the time I was walking back into town I was feeling decidedly itchy in unmentionable areas that I couldn't scratch in public!

I eventually found some unaffected trees and picked away, but I've moved the recipe here to try to catch the trees before the aphids.

No. of jars: 5 medium jars	Ingredients
	200g / 7oz lime tree blossoms, the leaves and buds
Time taken: 1 hour itching in the park, 1 hour sulking, then 3 hours	500ml / 2⅛ cup apple juice
	250ml / 1 cup Champagne or fizzy wine
	1 vanilla pod
	1kg / 5 cups jam sugar
	1 unwaxed lemon

How to Make

Stage 1

Add the lime tree blossoms and leaves to the jam pan or a large bowl.

Add the apple juice, champagne and ½ the vanilla pod.

Zest the lemon, add the zest and cut ½ of the lemon (pop the other half in the fridge) into slices and add.

Leave to stew overnight.

Stage 2

Prep your jars (cold oven 110°C / 225°F / Mk ¼ for 30 minutes) and lids, ladle and funnel (saucepan with boiling water for 20 seconds). Place 3 saucers in the fridge to test for set.

Place the juice in the jam pan. Add the juice of the remaining ½ lemon, scrape out the other half of the

vanilla pod and add that as well.

Warm the juice and add the jam sugar (or granulated sugar and pectin sachets, if using), stirring continuously until dissolved.

Increase the heat and look to set the jelly (or boil for a couple of minutes, take the jam pan off the heat and add the liquid pectin).

When you are happy with the set, ladle into jars and twist the lids on tightly.

Rhubarb Jam

YES, A REAL JAM! And it's not made with dried, frozen fruit, or canned fruit. It's made with fresh fruit, err... well a vegetable actually, but it marks the official start of JAMMY TIME.

I've been grooming the rhubarb at The Vege Place for some time. It sounds scary, but it's true. I've not used forced rhubarb as I hate the thought of violence on a poor vegetable. Really it just seems unnecessary to keep them warm in sheds when if you wait you can have outdoor rhubarb, which if they are anything like the tomatoes will taste better for it. No doubt it's the extra vim and vigour required to survive.

So I've been watching the outdoor rhubarb and keep saying to Regula, 'Do you think it's a bit dry? Might it need some water? Oh I will just go and check it.' At last the new shoots are thick and numerous enough for picking... and I'm off. I get that rhubarb home so fast my feet don't touch the ground. As I got a lift in a car they really didn't!

Buy or pick your rhubarb as fresh as possible so it won't be stringy and won't struggle to set. If your rhubarb is a little bendy then use jam sugar or add pectin, and if it's really long in the tooth, make rhubarb crumble.

No. of jars: 5½ medium jars, yielding about 1.8kg	Ingredients
Time taken: About 30 minutes chopping, then I left it to sit for 2½ hours, and then about 1 hour to heat to setting point. Approximately 4 hours in total	900g / 7½ cups diced rhubarb, home grown if possible
	900g / 4½ cups granulated sugar
	1 small lemon (2 tbsp juice)

How to Make

Stage 1

Cut off any rhubarb leaves and bin as these are poisonous, so you really don't want to eat them.

Rinse the rhubarb, cut into 2cm lengths and place in the jam pan.

Stir the sugar in, cover and leave to stand for a couple of hours or until water has been drawn out of the rhubarb.

Stage 2

Prep the jars (cold oven 110°C / 225°F / Mk ¼ for 30 minutes) and lids, ladle and funnel (saucepan with boiling water for 20 seconds). Place 3 saucers in the fridge to test for set.

Heat the rhubarb gently, stirring until the sugar has dissolved.

Add the lemon juice and bring to the boil.

Boil hard until setting point has been reached.

When you are happy with the set, ladle into the jars and twist the lids on tightly.

Place on a cake rack to cool then label and store.

Taste Test: Really, really good!! This is what it is all about. Steve put a smiley face on the side of several jars as he wants to keep them all. I've been so busy making marmalades we've run out of jam, and now everyone knows I make jam he can't really risk being caught going out and buying it.

Variations: Rhubarb and orange jam: Add the **zest of an orange** to the stewing fruit, and then add **orange juice** instead of the lemon juice after the sugar has dissolved.

Rhubarb and ginger jam: Add **1 tsp ground ginger** when adding the sugar or a little bit of the cheat's root ginger to give it a warming twang.

Fruity Things Learnt

My gung-ho approach to recipes doesn't always work. Slap-dash is rarely the best approach.

If the recipe really doesn't work it's not the end of the world. Particularly with unusual recipes, if there isn't time to make it again now, there's always time next year.

I know that sounds a bit final, but this is May and you need to get over it quick, because in June the summer fruit season truly explodes.

Useful Charts & Stuff

The following table gives the standard times for how long your preserves should keep - but they can vary quite a lot, so just use this as a rough guide.

Jams	1 year with a 1:1 ratio of sugar to fruit
	6 months with a 3:4 ratio of sugar to fruit
	Store in the fridge with a 1:2 ratio of sugar to fruit
Conserves	6 months
Jellies	1 year
Curds	3 months in a cool, dark cupboard with the full amount of sugar
Marmalade	1 year with a 1:1 ratio of sugar to fruit
	2 years if sugar to fruit is 2:1
Chutneys	2 years and keep for at least a month before opening
Fruits in alcohol	At least 6 months if filled right to the rim of the jar

I've divided my jars into small, medium and large. I have also become something of a 'jar junky.'

Large jars	450g
Medium jars	325g
Small jars	240g

Some recipes warm their sugar, why?

If you warm the sugar gently in the oven in an ovenproof dish it helps the sugar dissolve and helps avoids crystallisation. I'm too lazy to do this and find if you keep stirring the sugar it dissolves all by itself.

The following tables indicates which fruits are high, medium or low in pectin.

High	Apples (cooking and crab, the tarter the better = more acid), blackcurrants, citrus fruit peel and pith (lemons, limes, bitter oranges, grapefruit), damsons, gooseberries, plums (if slightly unripe, but they still like a bit of lemon juice), quinces, redcurrants, sloes and white currants
Medium	Apples (eating), apricots, blackberries, blueberries, cranberries, grapes, loganberries, medlars, plums (most) and sweet oranges
Low	Bananas, cherries, figs, haws, nectarines, passionfruit (high pectin if using the skin), peaches, pears, pineapples (strange but true), plums (when ripe), raspberries, rhubarb, rosehips and strawberries

Making Friends with Your Freezer

Ever since I nearly missed the Seville orange season (there are still so many jars of thick congealed brown stuff left in the cupboard – how could I forget), and realised I could freeze Seville oranges whole to use later, freezing suddenly seemed a whole lot more interesting. I'd started freezing over the summer, but it's only now that I'm pulling together some guidelines so my freezing technique isnt quite so hit and miss.

So give freezing a go. It prolongs the life of summer fruits and free fruits from the hedgerow which you can't even buy in the shops. Your frozen fruits can be used to make jams, jellies, curds and puddings, so all you need now is a little space in the freezer and to follow a few basic guidelines.

Freezing Etiquette

If possible pick and freeze your own fruit, then you can guarantee the quality and quantity. If not, try and buy the frozen fruit just after its season has ended from a farm shop or supermarket, looking out for freshly frozen.

Don't freeze knackered, bruised or battered fruit, freeze only the best. If you freeze over-ripe fruit, remember not to use it for jams and jellies as the pectin levels will be low, low, low, and it won't set. Probably the best way is to freeze it in a cooked fruit syrup. That way you won't try and use it for jam and it keeps better too.

You can freeze fruit in bags or containers. If the fruit is frozen in syrup, leave 2-3cm / 1 inch, (or one third of the pot) at the top of the container free for expansion. If the fruit is packed plain or just with a sugar sprinkle you don't need to do this.

Use frozen fruit straight from the freezer for jams or jellies, using 10% more fruit than a recipe states to make up for the loss of pectin. If you want to use fruit as a topping for a tart, defrost until just slightly frozen before using and drain off any excess water.

If fruit is frozen for too long it collapses a bit, fades and generally looks a bit dejected, so keep an eye on your freezer. If it's small like ours that's not a problem as we are always fighting for space.

Different Ways of Freezing Fruit

You can freeze fruit whole, peeled and sliced, in a sugar syrup, as a cooked or uncooked purée, a freezer jam or ready for action as a pie or pudding filling. Check out the following:

Freezing Whole Fruit

Seville oranges and all citrus fruit plus blackberries, blackcurrants (red and white are less firm and best as a purée), blueberries, figs, gooseberries, sloes, and basically all berries (apart from strawberries, and I'm not too sure about raspberries), can be frozen whole and kept in the freezer for up to 9 months.

The firmer the berry, the better it freezes. Some can even make 12 months, but that's pushing it. The flavour and texture might start to wane.

Fruit like strawberries, cherries and plums would be more like 6 months tops.

Just rinse and weigh the fruit, then mark the container or bag with the weight and date.

Freezing Sliced or Halved Fruit

Fruits like apples and pears (not quite as good) are best frozen peeled and sliced. Peel, place in a bowl of water with a squeeze of lemon juice to stop it going

187

brown, then slice, weigh / measure, lay on a tray, sprinkle with sugar (which helps it retain some of its texture), and place (still on the tray) in the freezer for about an hour. Once frozen, transfer to a weight and date marked bag or container. Fruits like plums and damsons can be cut in half, the stones removed, sprinkled with lemon juice and sugar and then frozen as with apples and pears. Fruit frozen like this keeps for up to 9 months.

Freezing Fruit in a Syrup

Syrups are good for freezing fruit to use for puddings and filling tarts. Some fruits are best preserved in a cold syrup while others are best lightly cooked in the syrup, then left to cool completely before being frozen. Read on for which syrup a fruit prefers, and bear in mind that some fruits are bi-lingual, or tri-lingual freezers – they can be frozen whole, sliced OR in a syrup.

Making a Syrup

Rinse the fruit in cold water, peel, stone, dice and slice, but be careful slicing as you don't want to end up with a pile of mush. Make a sugar syrup by dissolving **50g-300g / ¼- 1½ cups sugar** in **600ml / 2½ cups water**. The amount of sugar depends on whether you want a light or heavy syrup. **Caster / superfine sugar** dissolves best. Bring the water to the boil and stir until the sugar has dissolved. You need about **300ml / 1¼ cups syrup** for every **450g / 1lb fruit**.

Fruits best frozen in a cold syrup are blackberries, figs (whole or sliced) and rhubarb (blanch on its own for 2 minutes first, then leave to cool before adding the syrup). Just leave the syrup to cool completely before pouring over the prepped fruit and freezing. Sliced fruits keep for 9 months, the rest for 12 months.

Fruits best cooked in syrup then frozen are apples, pears, apricots, peaches and nectarines (but de-skin the last 3 in boiling water first), cherries (de-stone), quinces, greengages and plums, particularly damsons whose skins can toughen if uncooked. For fruits prone to discolouring add **a couple of tbsp lemon juice** to each **600ml / 2½ cups syrup**. Make the syrup, then cook the fruit in the syrup until it is just soft, allow to cool completely and freeze. These freeze for up to 9 months.

Fruit Purée

Fruits which freeze well as a purée include apples, pears and strawberries which can all be puréed with or without sugar, and apricots, peaches, nectarines (de-skin the last 3 in boiling water first), and greengages and plums which are best kept puréed with sugar, and red and white currants. Purée uncooked fruit with a little sugar and lemon juice and freeze for up to 6 months, or a cooked purée can be kept for up to 9 months. Again leave space for expansion. Purées are great for breakfast with yoghurt or stirred into porridge. The main fruit here is strawberries which don't freeze well any other way, which is why they are the main fruit for freezer jams.

Freezing Partly Cooked Fruit

I'm thinking apples. I've frozen them fully cooked for an apple crumble and also cooked for about 10 minutes in boiling water, sliced, drained, cooled and then frozen.

Freezing Fruit ready for Action

Fruit can be frozen with sugar, flour and flavourings ready to be defrosted for a pie or a pudding filling. I've frozen:

• Apple pie filling

- Sliced and de-stoned plums in a quantity for plum crumble cake (700g)

- Sliced apples uncooked, sprinkled with lemon juice, and topped with a crumble mix so that I can just defrost it and place straight in the oven.

Freezer Jams

Freezer jams are uncooked or lightly cooked and made with a lot less sugar, half to two thirds less than a normal jam. They only keep for 2 weeks once thawed, but keep for up to 6 months in the freezer, so give the taste of soft berry fruit long after the season has ended. Common freezer jam fruit includes blackberries, cherries, figs, raspberries and strawberries

Freezing Syrups

To freeze a syrup (not a fruit in a syrup) or a cordial (like elderflower cordial or rosehip syrup) you can fill plastic milk bottles and containers three quarters full, or freeze as ice cubes then decant into plastic bags to save space. You can then place an ice cube directly into a drink.

The Downsides of Freezing

Not the end of the world, but rather important for jam.

Freezing fruit destroys a little of the natural pectin in fruit as it breaks down the cell structure which stores the pectin. This is one of the reasons why adding sugar before freezing the fruit might help as it helps the fruit maintain its shape.

To make up for the loss of pectin when making jam from high pectin fruit, either add extra lemon juice, doubling the amount in the recipe, or add 2 tbsp of lemon juice for each 900g / 4½ cups of sugar OR freeze 10% more fruit than the recipe states. For example, most of the time I use about 900g of fruit for jam, so I freeze 1kg of fruit.

If making jam from frozen medium to low pectin fruit you definitely need to add pectin. Either use jam sugar or add ¾ of a bottle of liquid pectin plus the juice of 2 lemons, or 2 pectin sachets per 1kg of fruit used.

Other thoughts... The alternative to freezing is poaching fruit in syrup, which I haven't looked at in detail yet, as it requires heat processing / canning. Kitchen-wise I'm really not equipped for that yet.

Apricots, peaches and nectarines are better bottled than frozen, so I think next year I'm going to get into this, adding funky flavourings and making posh gifts, but not yet as it makes me all flustered at this moment.

A few FAQs

I've potted my jam, but it's not set.

If you've got an extra jar of preserve, you probably didn't boil off enough water, so empty it back into the jam pan and try for set again.

If you've got the correct number of jars then there wasn't enough pectin in the fruit. You can reset the jam, but the texture and taste won't be as good – think condensed sugar. So can you use the preserve as it is? If not you can empty it back into the jam pan with a bit of extra water and for each 1kg / 2lb 4oz of jam, add the juice of 2 lemons, a pectin sachet, or half a bottle of liquid pectin and 3 tbsp of lemon juice.

My curd has curdled – what can I do?

I say the curd, but I actually mean the eggs. Curdling can happen if the curd gets:

- Too hot if the mixing bowl touches the bottom of the saucepan or sits on the water, or if the water is boiling manically rather than simmering.

- Too acidic, for example if you've increased the fruit too much then it's an acid and egg shock.

- Or for some reason you will never discover, but you want to fix it.

- And sometimes it just looks like it's curdled as the butter hasn't actually finished melting.

Heroically save your curd by taking the curd bowl off the heat, and whisking vigorously until the mixture comes back together again, and then continue to cook as usual. Or add another egg to help rebalance the amount of tart juice. If by any horrible chance it doesn't come back together, either sieve your curd before potting, or make some kind of steamed pudding and claim it curdled whilst cooking.

Don't panic. Curdling must be rare as I've never done it, and I've made most common mistakes.

I want to make jam with my medium to low pectin fruit, but I can't find a recipe.

There are several different types of pectin pep-ups which will help your jam, jelly or conserve to set superfast.

For medium pectin fruit lemons are your flexible friend. Add them at the start if your fruit is low in acid and you want to help it release the pectin. Or add after the sugar has dissolved if your fruit just needs a little help to set.

For low pectin fruits use liquid pectin as well as your usual sugar and add it and a couple of tbsp lemon juice after the sugar has dissolved, and the jam has boiled rapidly for 3 or 4 minutes. You simply watch the jam thicken to set, re-heating only if necessary.

Or use powdered pectin which comes in packs of 3, usually in sachets for 1kg of fruit at a time. Add it with normal granulated sugar, then continue as usual.

Alternatively home-made pectin stock can be added after the fruit has softened, but just before adding the sugar. For a home-made pectin stock recipe see page 46.

When making jelly what's a 2nd straining of fruit?

If your fruit is high in pectin and not frozen, it's worth emptying the jelly bag back into the clean jam pan, adding about half as much water as the first time, heating the fruity pulp again and dripping it through the re-scalded jelly bag once more. This usually gets you about half the amount of juice as the first time, and you then mix this juice with the first amount of juice and proceed to make the jelly. Strangely redcurrants are no good as their flavour is too weak.